"Jann Aldr ~~~~~ ⅂itten a ground-breaking book that in ~~~~~ ⅂, the female personification of God, into all ~~~~~ ⅃ of Christian theology and life. She shows us that the Sophia understanding of God's presence in creation, revelation, and redemption underlay the original Christian understanding both of God's presence in creation and history as a whole and in Christ as the particular exemplar of this presence of God. A Sophia or Wisdom Christology reclaims the inclusivity of God and Christ in women and men and also in all creation. Sophia Christology also moves toward a transforming spirituality and understanding of the church's ministry and mission.

"Aldredge-Clanton concludes her book with helpful resources for worship across the church year read through the new eyes of Wisdom Christology. This is a 'must' book for all concerned with an inclusive and liberating theology and church."

Rosemary Radford Ruether
Georgia Harkness Professor of Applied Theology
Garrett-Evangelical Theological Seminary

"Dr. Aldredge-Clanton's unearthing of the Christ-Sophia provides a firm and reassuring foundation upon which true community can be built. Moving through the book, hope erupts eternal that Jew or Gentile, slave or free, male or female, *all* can truly be one in Christ-Sophia."

Cindy Johnson
Founder and Director
Bread for the Journey Proclamation Ministries

"Christ-Sophia. One days these words will seem just as natural as the phrase, Christ our Lord. That time will come because feminist scholars and practitioners, like Jann Aldredge-Clanton, will have contributed to a new understanding of God in the midst of a changing world.

"It is vitally important that all who are dedicated to doing the work of the church come to know and understand that it is salvific, not blasphemous, to pray to Christ-Sophia. If knowledge is power, as some say, then knowing Christ as Sophia offers access to a power capable of transforming us and our relationship to our world. This is serious, Spirit-led Christianity, and it is work that needs to be done.

"Aldredge-Clanton writes convincingly in a style and format that is accessible to people outside the academy, to those who fill the pulpits and pews and choir stalls on Sunday. The reflective questions will engage both the head and the heart, and be particularly effective when shared with a small Christian community within the congregation or with a circle of friends."

Miriam Therese Winter
Professor of Liturgy, Worship, Spirituality
Hartford Seminary, Hartford, CT

"This book is powerfully insightful and makes a significant contribution to the discussion/controversy regarding language about God. Aldredge-Clanton is equally painstaking both in her exploration of scripture and in her probing of human experience and motivation. I rejoice in her connection of injustice with the church's failure to grasp the power and meaning of resurrection."

Reverend Carolyn Bullard-Zerweck
Program Associate
Greater Dallas Community of Churches

In Search of the

CHRIST-SOPHIA

An Inclusive Christology for Liberating Christians

JANN ALDREDGE-CLANTON

XXIII

TWENTY-THIRD PUBLICATIONS
Mystic, CT 06355

Twenty-Third Publications
185 Willow Street
P.O. Box 180
Mystic, CT 06355
(203) 536-2611
800-321-0411

ISBN 0-89622-629-8
Library of Congress Catalog Card Number 94-61249
Printed in the U.S.A.

Acknowledgments

Many people helped me to bring the dream of this book into reality. I am grateful to my family who supported and nurtured me throughout the process. My sister Anne stretched my thinking and encouraged me to believe in my work. Her empowering support helped me persevere in following the Spirit within me. My husband David gave valuable technical assistance as well as loving support. My sons Brett and Chad stimulated my creativity and affirmed my goals. My mother Eva shared my struggles and successes along the way to completion.

The ideas and experiences of many people influenced the research and writing of this book. I have given credit to many of these in the endnotes. My dear friend Sally Browder played a major role in the conception of the book and made many creative contributions. As one of the founders of the Inclusive Worship Community, Sally helped create the experience which inspired the writing of this book. I am also grateful to Tom Artz, my editor at Twenty-Third Publications, for being an insightful, encouraging partner in the creative process.

My deep gratitude goes also to the participants in the Inclusive Worship Community who gathered from 1989 to 1993 in Waco, Texas, to envision new life: Rick Battistoni, Jay Belew, JoAnn Bristol, Sally Browder, Susan Cannon, Eugene Carter, Nancy Chinn, Katie Cook, Dan Danzeiser, Dawn Darwin, John DeVries, Dana Durham, Lisa Freeman, Robert Harris, Emma Harrison, Etta Hartfield, Lorine Hicks, Trish Holland, Nancy Larson, Lindsey Little, David Longfellow, Deirdre McClain, Donna McCune, Walter McDonald, Caroline McGee, Luther Mitchell, Jr., Tommye Mitchell, Rohndal Napier, Loretta Oliver, Jo Pendleton, Alberta Patterson, Jim Pettit, Betsy Ritz, Dinah Siemon, Randy Siemon, David Stricklin, Jean Batson Turner, Bob Uzzel, Debra Uzzel, Opal Watson, Ruth Williams, David Woody, Debra Woody.

CONTENTS

PART II:
CLAIMING THE POWER
OF THE RESURRECTED CHRIST-SOPHIA

PART III:
EXPERIENCING THE
RESURRECTED CHRIST-SOPHIA
THROUGH WORSHIP

Introduction

Can a woman be saved by a male Savior? This question poses a major challenge for contemporary Christians. Although theologians have examined this question for almost twenty years, lay people are only beginning to raise the issue. A little girl focuses the question more simply when she asks her mother, "Why wasn't Jesus born a girl instead of a boy?" Both male and female theologians and pastors concerned about justice and equality have responded with credible, creative answers.

Diane Tennis asserts that Jesus was male so that he could model servanthood, that "unlike women, he did not have to be a servant. He had power and access to power....Who but a man could credibly teach and model such a revolution in relationships by giving up power? Only a man could do that, because only men had power."[1] Brian Wren believes that Jesus was born male so that he could undermine the norms of patriarchal society and show Christian men that they must give up male power and privilege, thereby undermining the power and privilege of other males.[2] Miriam Therese Winter proposes that God took on flesh as a male "to witness to the value of the feminine, to teach men, through Jesus, that affirming the feminine is compatible with being a man, to teach us all, women and men, that true mutuality, true equality, is the core of the gospel's good news."[3]

Theologians have not always viewed the maleness of Jesus as support for egalitarianism. Many have contended that Jesus' maleness is the ultimate proof of a God-ordained patriarchal order. Thomas Aquinas, the most prolific and influential medieval theologian, declared that only a male could represent the fullness of human potential. Aquinas argued that the male is the normative human gender and that the female is by nature defective physically, morally, and mentally. For Aquinas, the incarnate Christ had to take the form of a male.[4]

The misogyny present in so much of the Christian tradition has led Naomi Goldenberg and others to declare Christianity irredeemable for women. Goldenberg says that a theology of women's liberation necessitates leaving Christ and the Bible behind. She asserts that the masculine image of Jesus Christ cannot possibly be a symbol for the liberation of women.[5] Not willing to reject Christianity outright, Sandra Schneiders believes that only by developing a creative and liberating christology can women have a future in institutional Christianity.[6]

Going a step beyond Schneiders, I believe we must develop a creative and liberating christology if Christianity is going to have a future for men as well as for women. The future of Christianity itself depends upon a christology that includes female, male, and all creation in new and empowering ways. For the liberation not only of women, but of men and all created beings, we need more than a masculine image of Christ.

In *The Quest of the Historical Jesus*, Albert Schweitzer examines the four gospels without finding a thread of connection by which to construct an accurate historical life of Jesus. He states that the biblical materials leave "yawning gaps," which theologians and historians have tried to fill. Schweitzer surveys biographies of Jesus written from the time of the eighteenth-century rationalists to early twentieth-century skeptics finding them to be based more on historical imagination and cultural biases than on authentic sources. Schweitzer concludes that those who have tried to formulate an accurate history of the life of Jesus have toiled in vain. Jesus cannot be contained in formulas and history books.[7] So said the writer of the Gospel of John: "But there are also many other things that Jesus did; if every one of them were written down, I suppose that the world itself could not contain the books that would be written" (Jn 21:25).[8]

Instead of despairing in his quest of the historical Jesus, Schweitzer discovers a more important concern: "It is not Jesus as historically known, but Jesus as spiritually arisen [within people], who is significant for our time and can help it." The power which can change the world is not the historical Jesus, but the Spirit going forth from Jesus into the lives of people. "The abiding and eternal in Jesus is absolutely independent of historical knowledge and can only be understood by contact with [Christ's Spirit] still at work in the world. In proportion as we have the Spirit of Jesus we have the true knowledge of Jesus."[9]

Creation theologian Matthew Fox believes that "religion would become an instrument of social awakening and deep social change for and by the masses if it let go of the quest for the historical Jesus and moved on to the quest for the Cosmic Christ." Fox goes on to say that today we need a "living Christ who can change history once again and ground that change in a living cosmology."[10] Cultural anthropologist and theologian Tom Driver believes that Christian feminism is possible only if "Christian doctrine can be freed from the hold of Christ past upon it while still remaining Christian." [11]

Daniel Migliore presents a contrasting viewpoint to Schweitzer, Fox, and Driver as he offers a word of caution against complete skepticism regarding historical knowledge of Jesus. Migliore finds agreement among current New Testament scholars concerning the centrality of Jesus' proclamation of the coming reign of God. The historical Jesus enacts this reign in an anticipatory way by his own love of God and his freedom to bless the poor, heal the sick, extend forgiveness to sinners, and liberate the oppressed.[12]

An authentic liberating christology must consider seriously the historical Jesus' proclamation in word and deed of the reign of God, but it cannot stop there. A liberating christology must move on from the saving truths discovered in the life of Jesus to a search for the risen Christ alive and active in the world today. This search is more than an academic pursuit. Christians go in search of the resurrected Christ not mainly for knowledge but for wisdom which comes through experience. They go in search of the risen Christ not only for the salvation of individuals, but for the salvation of the church and all of God's creation.

Central to the Christian faith is belief in the resurrection of Christ. The apostle Paul says that "if Christ has not been raised, then our proclamation has been in vain and your faith has been in vain" (1 Cor 15:14). Theologians and preachers for almost twenty centuries have debated the meaning of the resurrection. Some have made belief in the bodily resurrection a test of faith. But these debates and faith-tests have missed the point of the Christian faith in that they have emphasized belief in a doctrine instead of relationship to a person.

To relate to a personal Christ, Christians have to move Jesus from the distant past to the present day. Focus on the historical Jesus often obscures seeing the risen Christ in today's world. This over-emphasis on the historical Jesus constitutes one of the major theological problems for the Christian churches. When people make the historicity of the virgin birth, the historicity of the miracles, and the historicity of the resurrection their prime concerns, they miss the significance of the Christ-event. The resurrection is more than a historical fact to be affirmed. It proclaims the presence of God alive in the world today.

To limit Christ to the historical Jesus limits salvation to a short span of human history. Limiting Christ to the historical Jesus denies the resurrection. Jesus said to the disciples: "The one who believes in me will also do the works that I do and, in fact, will do greater works than these" (Jn 14:12). Jesus intended the work of salvation to continue and expand. The resurrection means that Christ is alive today and not limited to the particularity of one Jewish man living in Galilee almost two thousand years ago.

Many of the traditional hymns and prayers used in Christian worship services focus on the Jesus of the past, instead of opening the mind to discover the resurrected Christ at work in the world today. Referring to Christ exclusively in the masculine gender keeps the focus on the historical Jesus. A Christ who is exclusively "he," "king," "son," "master," "brother" cannot be the Christ who is alive in the world today. Limiting Christ to the masculine gender keeps Christ in history, denying the totality of the risen Christ. "And if Christ has not been raised, your faith is in vain" (1 Cor 15:17). In subtle ways, exclusively masculine language for Christ keeps us thinking about what Jesus did in the past rather than joining with Christ in transforming the world today.

Where do we find the resurrected Christ today? We begin by re-
calling the basic truth that Christ lives within all believers, female
and male. The mystery of Christ's indwelling is the "hope of glory"
(Col 1:27). Christ lives today in the Christian community, the Body
of Christ, made up of females and males. Paul tells the Corinthian
church, "Now you are the body of Christ and individually members
of it" (1 Cor 12:27). Christ can also be found in our sisters and brothers in need. Christ says: "As you did it to one of the least of these
who are members of my family, you did it to me" (Mt 25:40).

Limiting our thinking and speaking about Christ to the masculine gender diminishes the Christ indwelling in women. Roman
Catholics bar women from the priesthood because of the belief that
"Christ himself was and remains a man." If a woman performed the
priestly role, "it would be difficult to see in the minister the image
of Christ."[13] Seeing Christ in exclusively male images places external and internal limits on Christ's living within and ministering
through women.

Limiting our thinking and speaking about Christ to the masculine gender keeps us from a holistic picture of the Body of Christ,
presenting instead a picture of a male-only club. Furthermore, a
Christ who is always called "he" limits our ability to see Christ in
our hurting sisters as clearly as we see "him" in our brothers.

Adding feminine images and terms to the language used to describe Christ reinforces the universality of the resurrection by expressing the inclusivity of the biblical metaphors for the risen
Christ. Language that is inclusive of both female and male gender
more accurately represents the biblical images of the eternal Christ.
Biblical revelation and Christian tradition draw a parallel between
Christ and Wisdom, with the latter term being the feminine personification of God which is used throughout the Hebrew
Scriptures.

The apostle Paul calls Christ the "Wisdom of God" (1 Cor 1:24).
In the original Greek text the word for "wisdom" is the feminine
Sophia. The Gospels of Matthew and Luke compare Jesus to a moth-
er hen (Mt 23:37; Lk 13:34). In the middle ages, St. Anselm prays to
"Christ Mother"; Julian of Norwich praises Christ as "All-Wisdom,
our kindly Mother"; and Thomas Aquinas refers to Christ as "our
Mother, Wisdom of God."[14]

I propose the designation "Christ-Sophia" to express this theological truth. This designation, like all language used to denote and describe the deity, is metaphorical. No language can adequately express the fullness of the risen One. The metaphor "Christ-Sophia" is an attempt to give linguistic support to an inclusive christology. I am not suggesting a fourth person of the Trinity, but rather trying to recapture the lost feminine in the Second Person. Christ-Sophia does not replace the historical Jesus, but rather brings the truth taught and lived by Jesus into fuller reality. By adding "Sophia" and "She" to our language about Jesus the Christ, we will deepen our understanding of the eternal Christ and experience more fully the liberating power of the resurrected One in our world today.

This book seeks to balance a theological rationale for an inclusive christology with practical applications for Christian communities. Part One provides a theological foundation by defining Christ-Sophia (ch. 1) and then re-defining the doctrines of the pre-existence (ch. 2), the incarnation (ch. 3), and the resurrection of Christ (ch. 4) from the perspective of the Christ-Sophia. Part Two builds upon the theological foundation to claim the power of the resurrected Christ-Sophia for personal spirituality (ch. 5), social justice (ch. 6), and Christian community (ch. 7). Part Three provides additional insights for Christians seeking to integrate the theology of the Christ-Sophia into the setting of a worshiping community by offering appropriate liturgical resources for special seasons of the church year (ch. 8) and for other occasions (ch. 9).

PART I

Developing
a Theology
of the Resurrected
Christ-Sophia

CHAPTER 1

Who Is
Christ-Sophia?

Several of the New Testament writers link Jesus Christ to Wisdom, a personification of God in the Hebrew Scriptures. In Hebrew, the word for "Wisdom" is *Hokmah*. Not only is this term grammatically feminine, but the biblical depiction of *Hokmah* is also consistently female. The Book of Proverbs and other biblical wisdom literature describe *Hokmah* as sister, mother, female beloved, chef and hostess, preacher, judge, liberator, and establisher of justice. *Hokmah* exercises creative and redemptive power. She symbolizes female transcendent power pervading and ordering the world, leading nature and human beings along the right path to life.[1] *Hokmah* cherishes, exalts, and rewards those who are faithful to her:

> Get wisdom; get insight...Do not forsake her, and she will keep you; love her, and she will guard you. Prize her highly, and she will exalt you; she will honor you if you embrace her. She will place on your head a fair garland; she will bestow on you a beautiful crown. (Prv 4:5a, 6, 8–9)

In their attempts to express their experience of the saving significance of Jesus, New Testament writers found power in the Hebrew picture of *Hokmah*. The Greek word for *Hokmah* is the feminine *Sophia*. The apostle Paul refers to Christ as the *Sophia* of God:

"We proclaim Christ crucified, a stumbling block to Jews and foolishness to Gentiles, but to those who are called, both Jews and Greeks, Christ the power of God and the wisdom (*Sophia*) of God" (1 Cor 1:23–24). Proverbs describes *Hokmah* as the path, the knowledge, and the way that ensures life (Prv 4:11,22,26); the writer of the Gospel of John depicts Christ in parallel terms as "the way, and the truth, and the life" (Jn 14:6). What Judaism said of personified Wisdom (*Hokmah*), Christian writers came to say of Christ: the image of the invisible God (Col 1:15); the radiant light of God's glory (Heb 1:3); the firstborn of all creation (Col 1:15); the one through whom God created the world (Heb 1:2).

In much the same way that the Hebrew Scriptures characterized *Hokmah's* dealings with people, the gospel writers portrayed Jesus: calling out to the heavily burdened to come to him and find rest (Mt 11:28–30), making people friends of God (Jn 15:15), and giving life to those who love him (Jn 17:2).[2] In the Gospel of Matthew Jesus identifies with *Sophia* (Wisdom) when he says: "The Son of Man came eating and drinking, and they say, 'Look, a glutton and a drunkard, a friend of tax collectors and sinners!' Yet wisdom (*Sophia*) is vindicated by her deeds" (Mt 11:19).

The biblical connection between Jesus the Christ and divine Sophia provides the foundation for the designation of "Christ-Sophia." The next chapter of this book gives a more detailed examination of the biblical and historical identification of Sophia with Jesus.

The word *Sophia* suggests a person rather than an abstract concept and thus represents the biblical meaning more accurately than the word "wisdom." The biblical parallel between Christ and Sophia can be viewed as a symbol of the inclusiveness of Christ and of the liberating power of the resurrection. Bringing Christ-Sophia together linguistically helps Christians to internalize and appropriate this resurrection power.

Christ-Sophia reclaims a lost biblical image that holds the power to reveal a holistic picture of the liberating message of Christianity and to open new possibilities for a broader understanding of this central concept. In a discussion group dealing with gender issues, a history professor underscored the need for revising christological language. He pointed out that since the term "Christ" denotes a male figure to most people, using "Christ" to include female as well as male was similar to using the term "man" to include female as well as male. In both instances, the masculine takes on higher value as a universal category, while the feminine becomes devalued by exclusion.

For this reason this book advocates not only using female pronouns to refer to Christ, but also the inclusion of the feminine in the noun form. Christ-Sophia symbolizes linguistically the equal balance of male and female. As christology developed, the church ascribed the attributes and power of Sophia to Jesus in such a way as to repress the full richness of the image of Sophia.[3] The feminine dimension of Christ has thereby been separated from the masculine, and the meaning of Sophia has been lost.

Elisabeth and Jurgen Moltmann speak of Christ as "the human whose humanness was so long hidden under his maleness."[4] As long as Christians speak of Christ only in masculine terminology, Christ's humanness will remain hidden under maleness. By bringing Sophia and Christ together again, Christians can emphasize the wholeness of the incarnation and the liberation inherent in the resurrection.

The impact and implications of the image of Christ-Sophia for theological discourse and for Christian living and worship are both revolutionary and far-reaching. A few of those insights can be noted here while others will be developed throughout this book.

The image of Christ-Sophia can be used to modify the traditional images of the Creator of the universe. Christ-Sophia is the One who continually creates and re-creates, making "all things new" (Wis 7:27; Rev 21:5). Christ-Sophia is the author of all good things, even though she may not always be recognized as such: "In her company all good things came to me...but as yet I did not know she was their mother" (Wis 7:11–12). Recognizing Christ-Sophia as Creator challenges Christians to treat creation more wisely. If people see infinite Wisdom at the heart of creation, perhaps they will work harder to preserve the earth. Christ-Sophia theology celebrates the goodness of God's creation and the wisdom in caring for it. Christ-Sophia invites partnership in creation. All humanity, female and male, can become co-creators with Christ-Sophia.

Christ-Sophia also manifests more clearly the face of the divine Liberator. Humanity stands in need of liberation not only from personal sin, but also from sinful systems. It can be argued that Christian patriarchy is one of those sinful systems, and one that can only be liberated by a Christ who embodies the fullness of both male and female personhood. Rosemary Radford Ruether incisively demonstrates how exclusively masculine images of Christ continue to support male-dominated systems.

> Efforts to marginalize women in the Church and Christian so-ciety, to deprive them of voice, leadership, and authority, take the form of proclaiming that Christ was male and so only the male can "image" Christ. Woman, while the passive object of his redeeming work, can never actively represent him as medi-ator of God's word and deed. If feminist theology and spir-ituality decide that Christianity is irredeemable for women, its primary reason is likely to be this insurmountable block of a male Christ who fails to represent women.[5]

In the mind of many Christians, an exclusively male Christ con-tinues to be an insurmountable block to the liberation of both wom-en and men. This exclusive image of Christ distorts the Christ-event, taking one particular, time-limited trait of the historical Jesus and giving it universal, eternal meaning. The use of the image of Christ-Sophia brings liberation from these oppressive beliefs and systems.

Christ-Sophia reveals in new and profound ways the face of the divine Redeemer. Inclusive symbols for the divine, like Christ-Sophia, lend support to efforts intended to foster more egalitarian religious institutions. In a study of 174 men and women in six main-line denominations, 91% of those who imaged God as both male and female believed that women and men should serve equally in leadership positions in the church. Only 69% of those who imaged God as exclusively male believed the church should practice equal-ity in ministry.[6]

The image of Christ-Sophia also lends credibility to those intent on preserving the earth's resources as gifts of the loving Creator. The redemption achieved by Christ-Sophia extends beyond in-dividuals and institutions to all of creation. Thus the image of Christ-Sophia holds power to redeem sins against the earth.

Feminine christological language supports efforts to nurture the earth, traditionally referred to in feminine terms. Reclaiming the feminine in the symbolism for deity heightens awareness of the sacredness of non-human, as well as all human, creation. The efforts of the human community toward saving creation become a redemptive partnership with Christ-Sophia.

The image of Christ-Sophia also affects people's perception of their relationship to deity and to other people. Christ-Sophia illuminates the face of the divine as a friend. More and more individuals and organizations are realizing the efficacy of mutuality in relationships. Elinor Lenz and Barbara Myerhoff predict the eventual replacement of hierarchy with networks, which they see as "far better than the divisive pecking order of the hierarchical ladder."[7] Rosabeth Moss Kanter states that the new corporate ideal involves "partnerlike ties."[8] Churches are re-discovering the power of a "discipleship of equals called forth by Jesus."[9] Traditional christological images, such as master and Lord, subtly support hierarchical relationships; Christ-Sophia implies partnership, mutuality, and connectedness. While explicitly delineating the mutuality of male and female, Christ-Sophia implicitly models mutuality on all levels. Christ-Sophia encourages friendship and partnership, instead of dominance and submission, in Christian communities.

Christ-Sophia also reveals the authentic potential of humanity. In the beginning God created female and male equally in the divine image, and gave them equal responsibility for the rest of creation (Gen 1:27–28). One of the results of sin was a pattern of male-domination that destroyed this equal relation and limited human potential. Christ-Sophia came as Redeemer and Liberator from the bondage of sin. Christ-Sophia shows the full potential of male and female created in the image of God. Christ-Sophia models the glory of humankind and the abundant life for which all people are created (Jn 17:22; Jn 10:10).

Christ-Sophia includes and extends beyond the historical Jesus. Christ-Sophia is the eternal Word, equal to and partner with the Creator (Jn 1:1-3). Christ-Sophia became flesh in the historical Jesus so that people might see divine grace, truth, and glory in human form (Jn 1:14). In order to take on human form, Jesus had to accept restrictions of time, race, culture, and gender. But Christ-Sophia cannot be so restricted. Christ-Sophia rose from the dead, freed from all restrictions. "The understanding of Christ in terms of Sophia as the mediator in creation and as the power of the new creation underlines the cosmic significance of the Christian faith."[10]

Christ-Sophia brings the biblical christological metaphors to life. The New Testament pictures of Christ as the Spirit dwelling in individuals, as the corporate Body of believers, and as a person united with all suffering sisters and brothers come into sharper focus when they are seen through the image of Christ-Sophia. Including "Sophia" and "she" in contemporary christological language affirms in a new and powerful way the Christ who is alive in the hearts of female, as well as male, believers (Col 1:27). Including "she" and "Sophia" also affirms Christ alive in the whole Body of believers, women and men (1 Cor 12:27). Calling Christ "she" and "Sophia" opens our eyes to the Christ who is one with oppressed and suffering sisters, as well as brothers (Mt 25:40). Calling Christ "she" and "Sophia" and "Sister," as well as "he" and "Son" and "Brother," will authenticate the church's preaching and singing about Christ living in the world today.

Theologian Anne Carr holds that the reinterpretation of biblical images of Christ is necessary for the religious lives of contemporary Christian women. Such reinterpretation includes critical evaluation of the misuse of male symbols for Christ and the inclusion of female symbols, such as Sophia, for Christ.[11] This reinterpretation of theological images to include the feminine image is vital not only for the spirituality of women, but also for that of men. At stake is the survival not only of humanity but of the whole cosmos. Patriarchal christology has contributed to murderous crusades, witch burnings, slavery, anti-Semitism, abuse of women and men, and the rape of the earth.

In spite of efforts to enshrine male symbols for Christ, Christ-Sophia continually breaks through the stones and rises free of the limitations of gender, race, time, and ideology. Just as Western artists have overlooked the Jewish ancestry of Jesus and depicted him as light-skinned and blue-eyed in paintings and movies, Christ-Sophia likewise escapes cultural bondage. From the time of Constantine to modern-day America, political and ecclesiastical rulers have interpreted the principles of Christianity to sanction the system in power. Through liberation theology and practice, such as that of Gustavo Gutierrez, Christ-Sophia breaks through the stone of oppressive political systems in order to free oppressed people. Through creation theology, such as that of Matthew Fox, Christ-Sophia breaks through the social, political, and religious systems that destroy God's creation so as to free the whole cosmos. Through feminist theology, such as that of Rosemary Radford Ruether, Christ-Sophia breaks through the monolith of patriarchy in order to free women and all humanity.

Who is Christ-Sophia? Human language cannot adequately answer this question. Christ-Sophia cannot be contained in any human books or doctrines or institutions, yet Christ-Sophia became human flesh and lived among us, and thus can never be separated from humanity. This divine-human paradox in Christ-Sophia has challenged Christians beginning with the biblical writers through current theologians. Today Christians are being challenged to continue to expand their thinking and experience of Christ. If Christ can include both human and divine, surely Christ can include both male and female. Christ-Sophia invites people to a fuller discovery of the mystery inherent in the Christian faith.

In answer to Mary Daly and others who have declared Christianity and feminism incompatible, Marjorie Suchocki calls for a "christology which is neither sexist nor exploitable in sexist agendas." If we do not work toward such a christology, we will "leave the devastating effects of a male-dominated soteriology unchecked."[12] The image of Christ-Sophia developed in this book provides one among many efforts toward a christology which is liberating not only for women, but for all creation. The next three chapters focus on the eternal existence, the incarnation, and the resurrection of Christ-Sophia. Because christology focuses on a living person and not a static system, it continually grows beyond dogmatic pronouncements toward a fuller discovery of the way, the truth, and the life (Jn 14:6). This book encourages readers to make this discovery and to invite others to join the search for the resurrected Christ-Sophia who makes "all things new" (Rev 21:5).

QUESTIONS FOR
REFLECTION AND DISCUSSION

1. What are some parallels between Jesus Christ in the New Testament and Wisdom in the Hebrew Scriptures?

2. Do the names "Wisdom" and "Sophia" convey similar or different meanings to you? How do you feel when you use each one?

3. In what ways do exclusively masculine images of Christ support male-dominated churches and society?

4. Imagine what the world would have been like if Christ-Sophia had been the central image for Christians throughout history. How would things have been different?

5. In what ways does the name "Christ-Sophia" open possibilities of liberation and creativity?

6. How does the designation "Christ-Sophia" bring out the fullest meaning of the biblical christological metaphors?

7. What will inclusive christological symbols contribute to women, to men, to non-human life?

CHAPTER 2

Christ-Sophia
from the Beginning

My theological career began when I was a pre-schooler. I was the local sandbox theologian. One day my friend Philip, who was a year younger than I, asked me, "Who made this sand?" With confidence, I replied, "God made the sand and the trees and the flowers and everything." Philip held up a plastic bucket we were playing with and continued, "Who made this bucket?" I glibly answered, "People in a factory somewhere made the bucket, but God helped them make it." Philip persisted, "Well then who made God?" After a long pause and a deep sigh, I admitted, "Philip, I don't know everything!"

More than forty years later, with advanced degrees in theology and philosophy, I feel my limitations even more acutely. As a young girl, I pestered my parents and Sunday School teachers with questions like, "Where did God come from? How can God have always existed? Wasn't there some moment in time when God began to be?" Questions concerning the beginning of things have teased the wondering minds of bright-eyed children and professional theologians down through the centuries.

The Bible begins with "in the beginning" (Gen 1:1). The Gospel of John begins with "in the beginning" (Jn 1:1). These passages picture the beginning of the creation of the world. Scripture, however, does not answer questions concerning the beginning of God, but just states that God existed before anything else and that God created everything else.

Trinitarian theology developed as early Christians attempted to articulate their experiences of Jesus. Having experienced God's revelation through Jesus, they began to equate Jesus with God. They identified Jesus as the Christ. The Gospel of John calls Christ "the Word," who was one and the same as God from the beginning, and who created all things (Jn 1:1–3). Paul's letter to the Colossians also proclaims Christ to be active in creation from the beginning (Col 1:15–16).

The title "Christ" preceded the historical Jesus and was used to designate the Messiah, the one anointed by God to bring salvation, redemption, and liberation.[1] Without this understanding of Christ that antedated the historical Jesus, the reference in Hebrews to Moses' suffering abuse "for the Christ" (Heb 11:26) would be anachronistic. The writer of Hebrews, through this connection of Moses with Christ, indicates that suffering and liberation are always associated with the eternal Messiah, the Christ.[2]

Christian theology does not limit Christ to the lifetime of the historical Jesus. Christ, like God, is eternal, existing from the beginning and acting to begin creation. For many centuries after the life and death of Jesus, theologians debated and struggled with formulas and creeds to express the relationship between God and Christ. Logical formulas and doctrinal statements, however, could not express the indescribable Mystery that existed "in the beginning." The biblical writers used metaphorical language suggesting a variety of images.

THE IMAGE OF SOPHIA

The earliest picture the New Testament gives of Christ's existence from the beginning is that of Wisdom, or *Sophia*. The earliest christology to embrace the idea of pre-existence is Sophia christology. Early Christian hymns express Christ's pre-existence in the image of divine Sophia. Hebrews 1:1–3, Philippians 2:6–11, Colossians 1:15–17, and John 1:1–14 echo the language of biblical wisdom literature. Through applying wisdom imagery to Christ, these New Testament hymns stress the continuity between the person of Christ and God's creative, revelatory, and redemptive action. Christ alone so embodies Sophia that what can be said of Sophia can be said of Christ. In the early church the application of Sophia categories to Christ went hand-in-hand with the concept of the pre-existence of Christ.[3]

The description of the pre-existent Christ in many New Testament passages parallels the picture of Wisdom in the wisdom literature.[4] Both Christ and Wisdom existed before creation and participated in creation. Wisdom was "set up, at the first, before the beginning of the earth" (Prv 8:23), much as Christ was "before all things" (Col 1:17). In the beginning Wisdom took part in establishing "the heavens" and the "foundations of the earth" (Prv 8:27,28). Wisdom's creative power was all-inclusive: "Although alone, she can do all; herself unchanging, she makes all things new" (Wis 7:27).[5] Likewise Christ was "in the beginning with God," and "all things came into being through" Christ (Jn 1:2–3). Like Wisdom, Christ was the one "through whom" God "created the worlds" (Heb 1:2); in Christ "all things in heaven and on earth were created" (Col 1:16).

Christ and Wisdom both serve as the guiding truth for life. Proverbs pictures Wisdom as the path, the knowledge, and the way that insures life (Prv 4:11,22,26). Wisdom can teach truth "since she knows and understands everything" (Wis 9:10). Wisdom shows the way to life:

There is in her a spirit that is intelligent, holy, unique, manifold, subtle, mobile, clear, unpolluted, distinct, invulnerable, loving the good, keen, irresistible, beneficent, humane, steadfast, sure, free from anxiety, all-powerful, overseeing all, and penetrating through all spirits that are intelligent, pure, and altogether subtle. (Wis 7:22–23)

Likewise, the Gospel of John pictures Christ as "the way, and the truth, and the life" (Jn 14:6).

The New Testament depiction of Christ also parallels that of Wisdom in that both sustain the universe with order and goodness. Wisdom "deploys her strength from one end of the earth to the other, ordering all things for good" (Wis 8:1). From Wisdom comes "all good things" (Wis 7:11). Even so in Christ "all things hold together" (Col 1:17).

Biblical revelation pictures both Christ and Wisdom in the vital role of Redeemer. Throughout history "have the paths of those on earth been straightened...and saved, by Wisdom" (Wis 9:18). Chapter 10 of the book of Wisdom retells Israel's salvation history as the story of Sophia's redeeming power.[6] Her saving deeds were most dramatic during the Exodus: "A holy people and blameless race, this she delivered from a nation of oppressors....She brought them across the Red Sea, led them through that immensity of water" (Wis 10:15,18). In like fashion, Christ came not "to condemn the world, but in order that the world might be saved" (Jn 3:17).

What the biblical wisdom literature says of Wisdom, Paul and other New Testament writers say of Christ. The early Christians identified Christ as Sophia. The apostle Paul calls Christ the "Wisdom of God" (1 Cor 1:24), and says that Christ became for us "Wisdom from God" (1 Cor 1:30). Paul parallels Sophia and Christ when speaking of "God's Wisdom, secret and hidden" (1 Cor 2:7) and of Christ as "the revelation of the mystery that was kept secret for long ages" (Rom 16:25). Paul sees Christ as making known through the church "the Wisdom of God in its rich variety...to the rulers and authorities in the heavenly places" (Eph 3:10). To Paul, Christ is Sophia; thus Paul sees Christ as doing the work of Sophia.[7]

Paul indirectly identifies Christ with Sophia, when he says that the Israelites in the desert "drank from the spiritual rock that followed them, and the rock was Christ" (1 Cor 10:4). Hellenistic Jewish tradition linked the rock to the Wisdom of God, thus connecting the satisfaction of physical thirst through a well of water in a rock to the satisfaction of spiritual thirst through Wisdom.

Paul also suggests that Christ, like Sophia, serves as the mediator of creation, "through whom are all things and through whom we exist" (1 Cor 8:6). Paul thinks of Christ in terms of the personification of Sophia existing with God before the creation and active in creation.[8] Paul often states that baptized Christians have "put on Christ" (Gal 3:27), echoing Proverbs which admonishes people to embrace Wisdom (Prv 4:8). Just as embracing Wisdom brings unity, "putting on Christ" breaks down barriers of race, class, and gender: "There is neither Jew nor Greek, there is neither slave nor free, there is neither male nor female; for you are all one in Christ Jesus" (Gal 3:28, RSV).

Sophia christology pervades the early Christian missionary movement. The earliest theological interpretations of Jesus' life and death see Jesus as Sophia's messenger and later as Sophia herself. The earliest traditions connect Jesus with divine Sophia, the God of gracious goodness who accepts the poor and outcast. Wisdom literature depicts Sophia as sister, wife, mother, beloved, and teacher. She is the leader on the way, the preacher in Israel, and the Creator God. She seeks all people and invites them to dinner. She offers life, rest, knowledge, and salvation to those who accept her. Sophia officiates in the sanctuary and sends both prophets and apostles. The early Christians attributed all these characteristics of Sophia to Jesus. The connection of Jesus with Sophia, who wills the wholeness of everyone, enabled the earliest Christian communities to become a discipleship of equals.[9]

By the first half of the second century, the identification of Jesus as Sophia had become widespread.[10] Early Christians associated Jewish wisdom literature's personified Sophia with Jesus and absorbed part of a collection of wisdom sayings into a collection of Jesus sayings.[11] Many of Jesus' sayings in the synoptic gospels parallel material in Jewish wisdom literature.[12]

Jesus' description of love for the children of Israel in terms of a hen gathering her brood under her wings (Lk 13:34; Mt 23:37) parallels the tradition of Wisdom who continually calls people to share in her blessings and who wants her children to remain near her (Prv 8:32–35). Jesus seems to identify with pre-existent Sophia and to align himself with the prophets who appealed to the people in Wisdom's name and suffered rejection.[13] As the incarnation of the eternal Sophia, Jesus can say, as no merely historical person could: "How often have I desired to gather your children together as a hen gathers her brood under her wings, and you were not willing!" (Lk 13:34; Mt 23:37).[14]

Jesus also makes claims parallel to those of Wisdom: "Come to me, all you that are weary and are carrying heavy burdens, and I will give you rest. Take my yoke upon you, and learn from me; for I am gentle and humble in heart, and you will find rest for your souls. For my yoke is easy, and my burden is light" (Mt 11:28–30).

These words bear remarkable resemblance to two passages in Ecclesiasticus (Sirach) which refer to Wisdom: "Put your necks under her yoke, and let your souls receive instruction"; and "give your shoulder to her yoke...for in the end you will find rest in her" (Sir 51:26; 6:25,28). The Book of Proverbs portrays Wisdom as urging people to accept her teaching, but never making this teaching specific (Prv 8:1–21). The implication is that Wisdom is herself what is to be learned. Wisdom then becomes both teacher and that which is taught.[15] Jesus' invitation in Matthew chapter 11 is similar. Jesus is both teacher and the truth which is taught. The first person to issue this invitation is Sophia herself. Jesus, who is Sophia incarnate, re-issues her invitation.[16]

The Gospel of Matthew transforms a saying of Sophia recorded in the Gospel of Luke into a saying of Jesus. Luke's Gospel, probably nearer the original form, attributes these words to Sophia:

Therefore also the Wisdom (Sophia) of God said, "I will send them prophets and apostles, some of whom they will kill and persecute," so that this generation may be charged with the blood of all the prophets shed since the foundation of the world, from the blood of Abel to the blood of Zechariah, who perished between the altar and the sanctuary. Yes, I tell you, it will be charged against this generation. (Lk 11:49–51)

The Gospel of Matthew attributes almost identical words to Jesus:

Therefore I send you prophets, sages, and scribes, some of whom you will kill and crucify, and some you will flog in your synagogues and pursue from town to town, so that upon you may come all the righteous blood shed on earth, from the blood of righteous Abel to the blood of Zechariah son of Barachiah, whom you murdered between the sanctuary and the altar. Truly I tell you, all this will come upon this generation. (Mt 23:34–36)

In this Matthean passage, Jesus speaks not merely as the spokesperson for Sophia, but as Sophia herself.[17] Matthew assigns Sophia's function as the sender of prophets to Jesus, a function which belongs to no figure in pre-Christian Judaism except to Wisdom and to God. Matthew, like the apostle Paul, identifies Christ with Sophia against opponents for whom Jesus was but one of Sophia's messengers.[18]

In another passage in the Gospel of Matthew, Jesus clearly identifies with Sophia: "The Son of Man came eating and drinking, and they say, 'Look, a glutton and a drunkard, a friend of tax collectors and sinners!' Yet Wisdom [Sophia] is vindicated by her deeds" (Mt 11:19). The Gospel of Luke presents an earlier version of this saying: "Wisdom [Sophia] is vindicated by all her children" (Lk 7:35). Matthew's modification of the saying about Wisdom's "children" into one about Wisdom's "deeds" connects Jesus more closely with Wisdom. In Matthew's Gospel, Jesus is not just the last and greatest of Sophia's children, but is Sophia herself in the flesh. In other words, Jesus is not merely Sophia's child nor Sophia's prophet, but Sophia incarnate.[19]

These examples clearly demonstrate the biblical foundation for the designation "Christ-Sophia." New Testament writers regularly identified Christ as Sophia, the One who was present in the beginning and who remained active in creating and sustaining the world. Especially for Matthew, Paul, and John, speculation about the pre-existent Sophia constituted an important element in understanding Christ. They saw Jesus not only as bearer or speaker of wisdom, "but much more than that as Wisdom herself," as "pre-existent Wisdom Jesus Sophia."[20] New Testament writers groped for language to describe the "breadth and length and height and depth" (Eph 3:18) of their experience of Christ. They knew that this Christ preceded and exceeded the historical Jesus. The picture of pre-existent Sophia helped them express the eternal, cosmic significance of Christ. The picture of Christ-Sophia brought together creation and redemption, giving new and fuller expression to the liberating grace of God.

THE IMAGE OF THE LOGOS

The image of Christ as pre-existent Word (*Logos* in the original Greek) developed a little later than the image of Christ as pre-existent Sophia. Identification of Jesus as the incarnate Logos dominated the christology of the second and third centuries. Logos christology bridged the earliest Sophia christology of Paul and Matthew and the subsequent Son christology of the classic creeds.[21]

The Prologue of the Gospel of John draws the fullest biblical picture of the pre-existent Christ as Logos. The writer of John links the pre-existent Christ to the hellenistic concept of the eternal Word. Christ existed from the beginning with God as the Logos, or Word of God (Jn 1:1–2). Through the Word "all things came into being" (Jn 1:3). The opening words of the Gospel of John, "In the beginning was the Word" (Jn 1:1), parallel the opening words of the book of Genesis, "In the beginning God created the heavens and the earth" (Gen 1:1, RSV). John pictures Christ as the Word who spoke the world into existence and who revealed the way of God to the world. Christ as Word acted as both the agent of creation and of revelation about the cosmos and its creation.[22]

To the earliest readers of the Gospel of John, the Greek word *Logos* carried rich and complex connotations. No word in English can translate it adequately. It is like the concept of the Tao, or cosmic order, in Chinese philosophy. Logos includes the power that created and rules all of nature, God's plan for all of human history, and the moral law.[23]

In addition, the Greek concept of Logos implies that Christ is the rational mind and the structure of the universe. As early Christian philosophers pondered the connotations of Christ as eternal Logos, they realized the cosmological significance of reason in the framework of the doctrine of creation. The identification of the Logos as the rational principle of the cosmos acted to counteract the tendency in the early Christian movement to espouse the paradox of faith in Christ to the point of glorifying the irrational. Logos christology made it possible for those who accepted the paradox of faith in Christ to affirm also the validity of the rational process. The Christian could thus affirm the rationality of the cosmos and the legitimacy of the Christian's use of reason to grow in understanding of ultimate reality.[24] This use of reason is leading Christians today to see the irrationality of using exclusively masculine language to describe the cosmic Christ, the Logos.

Prejudice against women in the male-oriented society in which Christianity originated contributed to the exclusively masculine language used to describe the cosmic Logos. Greek philosophy in general and the neo-Platonic thought of Philo in particular influenced New Testament christology. Philo of Alexandria (ca. 20 B.C.E.-50 C.E.), the most influential and prolific author of hellenistic Judaism, contributed to the picture of the Logos as a masculine figure in the Prologue of the Gospel of John. Philo's belief that preeminence always belongs to the masculine influenced Christianity's repression of the feminine dimension of the divine. Philo used masculine images for what he believed to be the most valuable human and cultural qualities. In keeping with dualistic Greek philosophy, Philo separated body from spirit, equating the feminine with the physical and the masculine with the spiritual. Because he believed that the spiritual was superior to the physical, he also believed the masculine was superior to the feminine. Thus Philo refers to the cosmic Logos in masculine terms.

Philo equated the divine Logos and the divine Wisdom, seeing them as present with God and in God from the beginning.[25] Philo, however, transferred the attributes of the older, established figure of Sophia to a masculine Logos. His subordination of Sophia to Logos came from his desire to relate Jewish tradition to Greek philosophy as well as from his preference for masculine symbols. Further evidence of Philo's masculine bias occurred in his attribution of fatherhood to Sophia even though he admitted that her name is feminine. Believing that the feminine always falls short of the masculine, Philo tried to turn the unmistakably feminine Sophia into a masculine image of divinity. Philo's prejudice against the feminine contributed to the repression of the feminine dimension of the divine in Jewish and Christian theology.

The Logos in the Prologue of the Gospel of John is a masculine figure similar to the one developed by Philo. The Gospel of John takes the Greek neo-platonic Logos to new heights of divinization. Philo's influence contributed to John's transference of Sophia's power and attributes to the Logos.[26]

The Logos imagery in the Prologue of John draws heavily from pre-Christian wisdom speculation. Hebrew wisdom literature links "Wisdom" and "Word" in describing the creative power of God: "By the word of God the heavens were made" (Ps 33:6); "God by wisdom founded the earth" (Prv 3:19). The writer of the Book of

Hebrews also shows the combined influence of biblical wisdom theology and the Logos philosophy of Philo (Heb 1:1–3). Second-century Christian theologian Tertullian equates Wisdom with the Word, but gives greater emphasis to Christ as the Word. Tertullian's subordination of Sophia comes from the misogynism that led him to call women "the gateway of the devil."[27] Some other early Christian theologians distinguish between the Word and Wisdom by equating Wisdom with the Spirit of God and the Word more closely with Christ.[28] The title "Holy Spirit" is feminine in semitic languages, and at times is interchangeable with Sophia.[29] The disparagement and subordination of the female, along with the early subordination of the Holy Spirit within the Trinity, helps explain why Logos christology took precedence over Sophia christology.

By the fourth century it had become evident that of all the titles for Christ adopted during the first generations after Jesus, none was to have more momentous consequences than the title of Logos. In fact, Gregory of Nazianzus, an important Christian philosopher and theologian of that century, saw all other titles for Christ as predicates to the title of Logos. This title helped Christian philosophers to interpret Christ as the structure of reality and the answer to the riddle of being.[30]

THE IMAGE OF THE SON

Perhaps the most familiar image of the pre-existent Christ is that of the Son of God. But this concept was slow to develop. Only after the Council of Nicea in the fourth century did confession of Jesus Christ as Son become the standard formulation of Christian faith. Only in the conflict with Arius, a priest from Alexandria, did Logos christology give way to Son christology.[31] Arius taught that Christ was a created being and thus less than God who is the only uncreated, eternal Being. The Council of Nicea condemned Arianism as heresy, thereby affirming that Christ was of the same substance as God and thus equal to God. The church fathers who wrote the Nicene Creed used the designation "Son of God" to make their point that Christ was begotten, not created.[32] To establish what they considered orthodoxy, these theologians replaced the earlier titles of Sophia and Logos with Son of God.

The exclusive reciprocal relationship between Father and Son, however, has its basis in Sophia tradition. In biblical wisdom literature no one knows Sophia except God, and no one knows God except Sophia and those to whom she chooses to reveal God. In the book of Ecclesiasticus (Sirach) we find a description of this close relationship: "For whom has the root of Wisdom ever been uncovered? Her resourceful ways, who knows them? One only is wise, terrible indeed, seated on his throne, the Lord" (Sir 1:6,8). Matthew's Gospel records Jesus as saying: "No one knows the Son except the Father, and no one knows the Father except the Son and anyone to whom the Son chooses to reveal him" (Mt 11:27). This passage describes the Son in terms earlier scriptures reserved for Sophia herself. The Son has the same function as the heavenly Sophia, speaking as sole revealer and redeemer. The Son takes on the role of the divine Sophia as the sole mediator of the revelation of God.[33]

It stands to reason that the male-dominated society in which Christianity developed would gradually suppress the image of Christ as Sophia in favor of Christ as the Son. Furthermore, early Christian writers intended Son of God to designate relationship, not gender. Gregory of Nazianzus affirmed that the Trinitarian terms "Father" and "Son" did not indicate natures or essences or actions, but are metaphors for relations. The First Person of the Trinity is related to the Second Person as origin is related to that which is originated, as the one who begets is related to the begotten.[34] The faulty biology, along with the misogyny, of the early Christian theologians led them to ascribe all agency in procreation to the male partner. Thus they chose the term "Father" rather than "Mother" for the originating person of the Trinity. And because they wanted to affirm the absolute likeness and equality of the one originated to the originator, they called the Second Person of the Trinity, the "Son."[35] Their use of the word "beget," which connotes the father's rather than the mother's role in procreation, also evidences this patriarchal bias.

Another reason that Christians came to picture the Second Person of the Trinity as Son rather than Daughter was that Jesus was male. Traditional Christian creeds refer to Jesus as the Son of God incarnate. The creed approved as orthodox by the Council of Nicea in

325 and later affirmed by the Council of Chalcedon in 451 reveals the limitations of masculine language to make the very point they intended to make: that Christ, like God, is an uncreated, eternal Being:

> We believe...in one Lord Jesus Christ, the only-begotten Son of God, Begotten of the Father, before all the ages, Light of Light, true God of true God, begotten not made, of one substance with the Father, through whom all things were made; who for us men and for our salvation came down from the heavens, and was made flesh of the Holy Spirit and the Virgin Mary, and became man, and was crucified for us under Pontius Pilate, and suffered and was buried, and rose again on the third day according to the Scriptures, and ascended into the heavens, and sitteth on the right hand of the Father, and cometh again with glory to judge living and dead, of whose kingdom there shall be no end.[36]

The Apostles' Creed, still the most commonly used profession of faith in Christian churches, continues this same limitation by calling the eternal Christ God's only Son.[37] Not only modern Christian feminists, but also the early church fathers saw the theological inconsistency of attributing masculine gender to the Christ who existed before all the ages. If the Second Person of the Trinity is male, then the other two must be male as well, because the persons of the Trinity are the same in essence. The Second Person of the Trinity cannot be male unless God is male. Ambrose (339-397) and other early Christian theologians, however, affirmed the biblical truth that gender cannot be attributed to divinity because "God is spirit" (Jn 4:24). Christians came to call the Second Person of the Trinity "Son" because Jesus was male, not the other way around.[38]

The movement from Jesus' maleness to the concept of the Sonship of the Second Person of the Trinity appears to be an error of misplaced particularization. In other words, it lifts one particular trait of the historical Jesus into eternal divinity. If Christian theologians had exalted Jesus' race as they have Jesus' gender, then the Jewishness of Jesus would be reflected in trinitarian language. The patriarchal culture of the early Christian theologians who formulated trinitarian doctrine influenced the weight given the maleness of

Jesus in trinitarian language. There are no philosophical or theological grounds for the appropriation of male language into trinitarian doctrine.

The exclusive use of Father-Son language limits the expression of God's suffering, forgiving, and transformative love as revealed in the incarnate Christ.[39] Brian Wren colorfully expresses the limitations of the traditional designation of the Trinity as Father, Son, and Holy Spirit when he says that it "pictures God as an all-male one-parent family with a whoosh of vapor."[40] In order to communicate the universality of the eternal Christ, it is necessary to free language from the exclusivity of the masculine gender.

Contemporary Christian theologian Walter Kasper goes to great lengths to show that the pre-existence of Christ means God's eternal, universal concern for and activity on behalf of humankind. Without realizing it, however, Kasper sabotages this meaning through his exclusively masculine references:

> In the Son, God from eternity in freedom knows the sons; in the Son from eternity he is a God of men and for men. Here lies the profound meaning of the idea of the pre-existence of the Son. Far from being a purely speculative idea, it means that God as the God of Jesus Christ is a God of men who exists as eternally devoted to man.[41]

Kasper inadvertently but dramatically demonstrates how easily masculine references to God and Christ become translated into a religion of men and for men. If God is masculine, then God becomes a God of men who exists as eternally devoted to man. If Christ is a Son, then Christ knows the sons. If God in Christ is a Son from all eternity, then Christianity loses its universal meaning.

A NEW IMAGE

The Bible begins with a picture of God "in the beginning" giving birth to the universe (Gen 1:1), and ends with a vision of Christ as the "Alpha and the Omega, the beginning and the end" (Rev 21:6), proclaiming, "I am making all things new" (Rev 21:5). In the great mystery of the dawn of creation, God and Christ danced in creative unity. This divine creative activity did not stop, but continues in the present to make all things new.

Today it is not fanciful to say that the Spirit of Christ is inspiring the making of a new language to express the Christian faith. Because no language ever proves adequate to express God's revelation in Christ, new word pictures are always developing. Today's new pictures attempt to reveal a more universal image of God's creative and redemptive activity in Christ. The image of Christ-Sophia has a valid contribution to make in the formulation of new ways to speak about Christ and the entire Christian mystery. Christ-Sophia vividly pictures God's inclusive love for humankind. It transcends the alternative male-female symbolism of earlier pictures. The traditional designation "Christ" carries male connotations, while the name "Sophia" adds the feminine dimension to the picture. This combination promises fresh possibilities of inclusiveness for the Christian faith.

The picture of Christ-Sophia, in addition to being a new image, gathers up the earlier pictures of Christ as Wisdom, Logos, and Son. As has been demonstrated in this chapter, Scripture and Christian tradition have linked Wisdom, or Sophia, and Logos. Both picture Christ at the heart of creation. Both Sophia and Logos highlight the importance of reason in the Christian faith. Disciplined study of the cosmic order, or Logos, leads to Wisdom, or Sophia. The learning process then becomes a way for human beings to "become participants of the divine nature" (2 Pt 1:4) of Christ-Sophia. We have also seen the biblical connection between the pictures of Sophia and Son in relationship to God. Both bring into focus the Second Person of the Trinity as revealer, mediator, and redeemer.

When the title "Son" replaced the title "Sophia," the church lost important dimensions of the Christ-image. Bringing back the picture of Sophia in relationship to the eternal Christ will not only bring balance in gender, but will also provide a more accurate picture of Scripture and of early Christianity. The image of God in the Hebrew Scriptures which had the most comprehensive influence on the early church's understanding of Jesus was the feminine figure of Holy Wisdom.[42] This image of Wisdom helped the early church connect Jesus with the eternal God, who was "in the beginning." Influential second-century theologian Justin Martyr finds the word

"Wisdom" most accurate in referring to the eternal Second Person of the Trinity. Justin asserts that Christ, "who is called Wisdom by Solomon, was begotten, both as a beginning...and an offspring by God."[43] Origen, another important early Christian theologian, equates Sophia with Christ, stating that Wisdom is the most ancient and most appropriate title given to Jesus.[44]

The title "Christ-Sophia" provides a theologically accurate picture for the Second Person present from the beginning with the First Person of the Trinity. Christ "is the image of the invisible God" (Col 1:15). Christ "is the reflection of God's glory and the exact imprint of God's very being" (Heb 1:2–3). Since Christ is an exact reproduction of God, then Christ, like God, includes female as well as male. Along with masculine images of God, the Bible gives us feminine images of God, such as comforting mother (Is 66:13), mother eagle (Dt 32:11–12), bereaved mother bear (Hos 13:6), woman in labor (Is 42:14), nursing mother (Is 49:15), midwife (Ps 22:9–10), Lady Wisdom (Prv 1,4,8), woman searching for a lost coin (Lk 15:8–10), woman making bread (Lk 13:20–21), and many others.[45] Therefore, since Christ images the invisible God, then Christ includes all these feminine images of God, along with the masculine images.

Why then has traditional Christian theology limited the eternal Christ, present and active with God from the beginning of creation, through images drawn from only one human gender? One explanation lies in the sin of pride. Reinhold Niebuhr finds the biblical definition of basic sin to be pride. Niebuhr believes that the religious dimension of this pride is humanity's "effort to usurp the place of God," and that the "moral and social dimension...is injustice. The ego which falsely makes itself the centre of existence in its pride and will-to-power inevitably subordinates other life to its will and thus does injustice to other life."[46] Insistence on male terms for the deity might be linked to this pride which seeks to usurp divine power and to subordinate other people. Today Wisdom is leading the Christian community to see the sinfulness, the biblical inaccuracy, and the logical fallacy of an exclusively masculine theological language. The image of Christ-Sophia clearly reflects the theology of an eternal Christ who became flesh to liberate the oppressed. It also champions the belief that the Christian message is rooted in an inclusive gospel (Gal 3:28).

The new picture of Christ-Sophia will bring good news not only for human beings, but for the whole cosmos. Matthew Fox links Wisdom and Mother Earth, lamenting that both are dying. "Wisdom appears universally in cultures and religions as a feminine, maternal figure. And wisdom is dying." Wisdom is "linked with our learning of and relating to the ways of the cosmos."[47] The restoration of the feminine image of Wisdom becomes vital to the survival of the cosmos.[48] Fox thus integrates the feminine into his picture of the cosmic Christ. The title "Christ-Sophia" provides a more accurate linguistic representation of this integration.

No human words or pictures can contain the creative mystery that began "the heavens and the earth" (Gen 1:1). No human logic can provide answers to questions concerning the beginning of the One who began it all. But Wisdom is leading Christians to expand their vision of divine beginnings in order to restore human relationships and the whole cosmic order. Christ-Sophia from the beginning created the good and the beautiful cosmos. In the beginning, human beings lived in mutual, loving relationship. Human and non-human creation lived in harmony and blessedness. The new image of Christ-Sophia can help Christians see this harmonious creation as the divine intention from the beginning.

QUESTIONS FOR REFLECTION AND DISCUSSION

1. When you try to imagine the beginning of the universe, how do you picture the creator?

2. How did the early Christians draw from biblical wisdom literature in their attempts to express the pre-existence of Christ?

3. Which one of Paul's parallels between Christ and Sophia holds the most meaning for you?

4. In what ways does Jesus identify with Sophia?

5. How did the cosmic Logos come to be described in masculine terms?

6. Why do you think that by the fourth-century Logos christology had taken precedence over Sophia christology?

7. Why do you think that the image of Christ as Son took precedence over the images of Christ as Sophia and as Logos?

8. How would Christianity have been different if the Second Person of the Trinity had been referred to as "Daughter" instead of "Son"?

9. In what ways is the new image of Christ-Sophia more theologically accurate than other images presented in this chapter? What other christological images would you propose to convey the universality of divine creative and redemptive activity?

10. What feelings does the new image of Christ-Sophia evoke in you?

CHAPTER 3

Christ-Sophia in the Flesh of Jesus

In a class discussing the book *In Whose Image? God and Gender,* a lively interchange developed on such issues as men's feelings toward women in authority, women's feelings toward male and female professionals, and the connections between sexism and racism. One man told about his experience of feeling nurtured as he was guided by a female counseling supervisor. One woman compared her experiences with male and female doctors. Finally someone near the back of the room blurted out, "I thought we were supposed to be talking about God and how we think and speak about God. You all keep getting off the track, talking about your own experiences."

Although Christians profess belief in the incarnation, they do not always understand the implications of incarnational theology and what it means to talk about God in human flesh. Incarnational theology intimately links God with human experience. As Edward Schillebeeckx says, "Belief in God is impossible without belief in humanity."[1] The mystery of the incarnation focuses on the paradox of divinity and humanity united in God.

Theologians have long maintained that God transcends sexuality and gender, and that the humanity of Jesus, not his maleness, is central to the Christian understanding of the incarnation. But these theological distinctions have little impact on the way the symbols of Father and Son actually function to support religious and cultural ideologies that cripple women.[2] For example, some Christians still use the image of God as Father to enforce the dominance of fathers in the home and men in society, thereby contributing to the abuse of women and children. Others use Jesus' maleness to validate an all-male priesthood.

Jesus' actions and words, however, gave no support to male dominance. Rather Jesus challenged this oppressive social structure, advanced the role of women, and embodied personal and emotional traits stereotypically attributed to women. Christ-Sophia became flesh in Jesus to lead the way to liberation and justice.

JESUS' FEMINIST ACTIONS

Although the religious establishment of Jesus' day sought a warrior-king Messiah, Jesus took the role of suffering servant (Phil 2:6–8). Jesus reversed the norms of hierarchical society and routinely shocked his disciples who behaved according to their socialization as males. When they competed for the position of the greatest, Jesus told them that greatness comes from serving, not from lording it over others. Jesus further startled them by identifying with a child, who in patriarchal society had even less value than a woman. Jesus declared, "Whoever welcomes one such child in my name welcomes me" (Mk 9:37). In Matthew's Gospel, the mother of two disciples asked Jesus for top positions for her sons. This mother sought power and status in the only way open to her in that society: through the men related to her. Again Jesus spoke of a different kind of power, the power of servanthood: "Whoever wishes to be great among you must be your servant" (Mt 20:26).

Jesus taught that this kind of servanthood did not keep people down, but lifted them up. Too often women in Christian churches have taken Jesus' teaching of servanthood to the extreme to glorify their secondary status, while men have applauded the notion of servanthood for themselves in theory, but in practice have used it to subordinate women. Jesus taught and demonstrated a servanthood that was not "simply an acceptance of the servile status of the humble in present society."[3] Rather it completely destroyed one-up, one-down relationships by encouraging the most able people to offer their services freely to those in need of them. The kind of servanthood that Jesus taught is possible only for liberated individuals. It exercises power and leadership not to make others dependent, but to empower and liberate others.[4] Jesus' style of servanthood led to the reciprocal, egalitarian community of the early church described in Acts: "All who believed were together and had all things in common; they would sell their possessions and goods and distribute the proceeds to all, as any had need" (Acts 2:44–45).

The gospel accounts reveal that Jesus modeled egalitarian relationships between men and women. He went beyond a paternalistic kindness and consideration of women and completely rejected the chauvinism intrinsic to male-dominated culture. Jesus radically challenged the social structures of his culture and the social injustices intrinsic to those structures. In word and deed Jesus called for a revolutionary liberation of the human, social, and cultural order.[5]

Contrary to the popular belief that feminists are all radical women, some of the best and most active feminists are men. As Jesus demonstrated, men can be powerful feminists because they work from a position of power and a willingness to give up power for the good of all humanity. Linda Ellerbee says that being "feminist doesn't mean turning the tables on men, but throwing out all tables except round tables."[6] Sandra Schneiders defines a feminist as "a person who believes in the full personhood and equality of women and who acts to bring that belief to the realization of society and church."[7] Even though "feminist" is a modern designation, it can apply to Jesus in the light of these definitions.

Leonard Swidler places Jesus in the context of feminism when he writes: "Feminism, that is, personalism extended to women, is a constitutive part of the gospel, the good news, of Jesus."[8] Back in 1947, Dorothy Sayers eloquently captured this feminism of Jesus:

Perhaps it is no wonder that the women were first at the Cradle and last at the Cross. They had never known a man like this Man—there never has been such another. A prophet and teacher who never nagged at them, never flattered or coaxed or patronised; who never made arch jokes about them, never treated them either as "The women, God help us!" or "The ladies, God bless them!"; who rebuked without querulousness and praised without condescension; who took their questions and arguments seriously; who never mapped out their sphere for them, never urged them to be feminine or jeered at them for being female; who had no axe to grind and no uneasy male dignity to defend; who took them as he found them and was completely unself-conscious. There is no act, no sermon, no parable in the whole Gospel that borrows its pungency from female perversity; nobody could possibly guess from the words and deeds of Jesus that there was anything "funny" about women's nature.[9]

Jesus related to women with complete naturalness and spontaneous matter-of-factness. He addressed women and men as equals and replaced "all the values of this male-shaped world based on achievement, property, and action" with the "receptive, tolerating, open methods of being most often embodied by women."[10] Over against the patriarchalism of his own day and even measured against contemporary standards, Jesus as revealed in the gospels is remarkably nonsexist and inclusive.

In the light of the male-dominance of Jewish and Christian traditions, Jesus' actions stand out more clearly as feminist. Jewish oral tradition held that the testimony of one hundred women was not equal to that of one man. Women received harsher sentences for adultery than men (Num 5:11–31), and had no rights of inheritance if there were male heirs (Num 27:1–11). It is little wonder that oral tradition declared, "Woe unto him whose children are females." Women did not even have freedom in religious matters. A father or husband could veto a woman's religious vows (Num 30:3–15). Similar attitudes and practices developed in the Christian community: "Let a woman learn in silence with full submission. I permit no woman to teach or to have authority over a man; she is to keep silent. For Adam was formed first, then Eve; and Adam was not deceived, but the woman was deceived and became a transgressor" (1 Tm 2:11–12). The writer of First Peter speaks of "woman as the weaker sex" (1 Pt 3:7). Christian wives were to subject themselves to their husbands, just as slaves obeyed their masters (Eph 5:22; 6:5). Saint Augustine, the most influential theologian of the early church, contradicts Genesis 1:27 by denying that women are created in the image of God. Thomas Aquinas, the medieval theologian whose influence continues to shape Christianity, declared that females are defective: "For the active power in the seed of the male tends to produce something like itself, perfect in masculinity; but the procreation of a female [results from some] debility of the active power [or] some unsuitability of the material."[11]

In contrast to such statements, Jesus' feminism was indeed radical. Jesus' attitude toward women would be revolutionary even for today.[12] He placed equal value on women and men, and demonstrated that women are worthy and capable of understanding the mysteries of the faith. Jesus gave Mary of Bethany the role of disciple-learner. Breaking a rule against rabbis teaching women, Jesus taught Mary and commended her for choosing the non-traditional role of theology student (Lk 10:39–42). In so doing, Jesus affirmed the ministry of proclaiming the word for women.[13]

Contrary to the common belief that Jesus chose only male disciples, the Bible tells the story of female disciples as well. Women, as well as men, followed Jesus as disciples. Mary Magdalene, Joanna, Susanna, Mary the mother of James and Joseph, Salome, and many others followed Jesus and ministered to him (Lk 8:1–3; Mk 15:40–41; Mt 27:55–56). It was unheard of for a Jewish woman to leave home and travel with a rabbi, but Jesus broke this cultural custom by calling these women to travel openly with him.[14] By calling women to be disciples and to travel with him, Jesus affirmed women in a new and startling manner.

Jesus never related to his female disciples with condescending chivalry or with paternalism. He reached out to these women in order to help them and to be helped by them. He valued their gifts knowing that he needed them. Jesus gladly accepted the ministry of women. All three synoptic gospels use a form of the Greek verb *diakoneo* (to minister or be a deacon) to describe what these women did for Jesus. At the time of the crucifixion and resurrection, the ministry of these female disciples became invaluable gifts to Jesus. In these actions Jesus served as a model for male feminists who advocate equality for women not just for the sake of women, but for the sake of men as well.

Jesus further demonstrated the great value he placed on women's spiritual and intellectual gifts in selecting witnesses to his messianic mission and his resurrection. The Gospel of John records Jesus' announcing his messianic mission first to the Samaritan woman (Jn 4:7–26). In all four gospel accounts, we find Mary Magdalene and other women as the first witnesses of the empty tomb. Although the religious establishment of that day did not think women worthy to learn anything about religion, Jesus trusted these most important spiritual truths to women.

Jesus valued the gifts of the Samaritan woman more highly than he respected the traditional religious views concerning relationships between men and women and between races. In relating to the Samaritan woman, Jesus broke racial and gender taboos that were as strong as the racial tension between blacks and whites in the segregated South. Jews and Samaritans avoided any contact with one another. By initiating a conversation with a Samaritan woman, Jesus flagrantly violated tradition on two counts: He spoke to a Samaritan and to a woman. The woman expressed her consternation at both violations: "How is it that you, a Jew, ask a drink of me, a woman of Samaria?" (Jn 4:9). John notes that Jesus' speaking with a woman was an even more shocking breach of tradition than his speaking with a Samaritan: "Just then his disciples came. They were astonished that he was speaking with a woman" (Jn 4:27).

Jesus further undermined patriarchal standards by valuing this Samaritan woman for who she was as an individual, instead of for who she was in relationship to men. Jesus made a point of letting her know that her relationships to men had nothing to do with her worthiness to receive and proclaim spiritual truths. Jesus quickly moved from her five husbands and current illicit relationship to discuss with her the most profound truths concerning worship and God's nature. Then Jesus revealed his messianic mission to this woman of Samaria. By choosing her as the first person to receive the messianic announcement, Jesus completely reversed the racial and gender values of his culture. Despite the fact that society labeled the Samaritan woman unfit by race, gender, and morality to handle holy matters, Jesus trusted this woman with the sacred task of spreading the news about his identity (Jn 4:26–39).

The church's treatment of Mary Magdalene reflects its traditional devaluing of women. All four gospel accounts clearly state that Mary Magdalene and other women were the first to witness the empty tomb (Mt 28:1–10; Mk 16:1–8; Lk 24:1–11; Jn 20:1–18). According to the Gospel of Matthew, after the resurrection Jesus first met Mary Magdalene and "the other Mary" and sent them as witnesses to the male disciples. The Gospel of John emphasizes Jesus' first resurrection appearance to Mary Magdalene and Jesus' command to her to instruct the male disciples concerning his ascension. Jesus' actions recorded here were such a shocking breach of tradition that they have often been discounted or ignored. In Luke's Gospel we find the first discounting of the women's testimony: "Now it was Mary Magdalene, Joanna, and Mary the mother of James, and the other women with them who told this to the apostles. But these words seemed to them an idle tale, and they did not believe them" (24:10–11). The apostle Paul totally ignores the prominent role Jesus gave to Mary Magdalene and the other female disciples. Paul states that Jesus appeared first to Peter and then to the twelve male disciples (1 Cor 15:3–5). Paul never refers to Jesus' appearance to Mary Magdalene or to the other female disciples.

Many people who could not ignore Jesus' appearance to Mary Magdalene have tried to discredit her. Beginning with the apostles who called her words an idle tale, theologians have questioned her sanity and her morals. The only biblical basis for attributing mental illness to Mary Magdalene is Luke 8:2 and Mark 16:9, the latter of which in not included in the oldest and most reliable manuscripts. If Luke's mention of her "evil spirits and infirmities" is indicative of mental illness, one cannot overlook the more important fact that Jesus healed her of this condition. As to her morals, church tradition has falsely depicted her as a prostitute. Attempts to identify her with the sinful woman of Luke 7:37–50 are totally unfounded. All the references to Mary Magdalene in the gospels, except that in Luke chapter 8, show her prominent ministerial role at the crucifixion and resurrection of Jesus.[15] Even the passage in Luke emphasizes her importance as a disciple and minister, not her "infirmities." Nowhere does the Bible indicate that Mary Magdalene was a prostitute. The traditional disparagement of Mary Magdalene highlights the radical nature of Jesus' choice of a woman as the apostle to the apostles, the one sent to bear witness of the resurrection to the male apostles. Down through the centuries the church has choked on this radically feminist act of Jesus.

Christian tradition has also discounted the value Jesus placed on the confession of Martha (Jn 11:27). Martha's confession that Jesus is the Christ parallels that of Peter (Mt 16:16). Jesus trusted Martha's spiritual insight enough to challenge her to make this confession of faith, just as he challenged the male disciples at Caesarea Philippi. Martha's statement is a christological confession in the fuller Johannine messianic sense of Jesus as the revealer come down from heaven. Just as Peter represents the apostolic faith of the Matthean community, so Martha represents the full apostolic faith of the Johannine community.[16] Martha's confession is equal to Peter's in theological significance.[17] Christian churches, however, have placed little emphasis on Martha's confession. Roman Catholic tradition has interpreted the confession of Peter as the basis for giving him and his male successors the authoritative leadership of the church. If this tradition had taken Martha's confession of faith as seriously as Peter's, there would have been female as well as male popes.

In reaching out to women and recognizing their dignity as people created in the image of God, Jesus also challenged the religious bias that barred a woman from sacred experience because of her physical processes. Levitical law stated that a woman with a discharge of blood, whether menstrual or otherwise, was ritually unclean (Lv 15:19–30). She could not participate in any worship services. Anyone or anything she touched, or anyone who touched her, became unclean. Instead of viewing menstruation as a part of God's good creation, Levitical law labeled it as dirty and sinful, and extended these labels to women themselves. Jesus challenged such labels and made a point of letting the large crowd of people know that this so-called unclean woman had touched him. Then instead of being rendered unclean, Jesus healed the woman. Jesus shifted the focus away from the woman's physical condition to her spiritual power and dignity. Jesus gave the woman and her faith credit for the healing (Mk 5:24–34; Mt 9:20–22).

Lest people think that prejudice against women because of their physical functions is a thing of the past, one need only to listen to some current objections to women pastors. One Protestant leader argues against women pastors, saying, "A pregnant woman can't baptize." Jesus, on the other hand, never used women's physical nature to limit them in any way. Rejecting the bias that views women as sexual objects, Jesus related to women as whole persons.

One day Jesus preached a sermon which deeply moved a woman in the crowd. Imagining how happy she would be to have a son like Jesus, she cried out: "Blessed is the womb that bore you, and the breasts that nursed you!" (Lk 11:27). Having thoroughly internalized the prejudices of her society that reduced women to wombs and breasts, the woman believed that she was paying a high compliment both to Jesus and to his mother. Jesus, however, rejected this "baby machine" image of women and insisted on human personhood, an individual's intellectual and spiritual faculties, as primary for all.[18] Jesus replied to the woman's outburst: "Blessed rather are those who hear the word of God and obey it!" (Lk 11:28). The church still has not fully applied Jesus' plain teaching in this text: Women are more than their sexuality.

Jesus also defied patriarchal custom in the way he related to the woman who anointed him with costly perfume. Jesus' culture did not allow women even to enter the dining area where men were eating. But Jesus welcomed the woman who burst into the gathering of men at Bethany in the home of Simon the leper (Mk 14:3–9; Mt 26:6–13). While some of those present sharply criticized this woman for wasting expensive perfumed oil, Jesus accepted and praised her act of spontaneous love. Instead of buying into their pragmatic economic value system, Jesus affirmed her appreciation of beauty for its own sake. He called her act a "beautiful thing," and said that "wherever the good news is proclaimed in the whole world, what she has done will be told in remembrance of her" (Mk 14:6,9).

The church has not faithfully told the story of this woman's beautiful act. Even though there is striking similarity between Jesus' words, "What she has done will be told in remembrance of her," and his words at the last supper, "Do this in remembrance of me" (Lk 22:19), Christians have not told this woman's story with even a fraction of the fidelity they have given to the Last Supper.[19] The Christian churches have chosen not to remember the feminine in Jesus or Jesus' affirmation of the feminine. Like Martha's confession of faith, this woman's act of love, so highly praised by Jesus, has been ignored or marginalized by the institutional church. Church tradition has negated things "in remembrance of her." But Jesus exalted the memory of "her."

JESUS' FEMINIST WORDS

Although Jesus' language could not be called inclusive by today's standards, it was radical for the culture of the day. Jesus included women in his illustrations and teachings, a practice unusual and surprising for that culture. Not only did Jesus include women, but he included them in positive, often exalted ways. His references to women always showed respect. Jesus demonstrated feminist inclusiveness in balancing stories featuring men with stories featuring women. It is obvious that Jesus' teaching was for both women and men.

Jesus' main message concerned the reign of God (Mk 1:15; Mt 4:17). Although Jesus left the meaning of the reign of God open to interpretation, most interpreters connect it to the Jewish concept of *shalom*. The reign of God, like *shalom*, means peace between nations, between individuals, within individuals, and in the whole cosmos. Jesus' message of the coming of the reign of God can be seen in the context of humanity's search for peace, freedom, justice, and life. This reign of God brings salvation from the forces of evil which are hostile to creation, as well as liberation of human beings to become all God created them to be.[20] Jesus' preaching of the reign of God challenged the forces of oppression and affirmed the full personhood and equality of women and men. Jesus' main message thus included issues related to feminism.

In preaching this central message of the reign of God, Jesus gave equal value to men and women through his illustrations. Jesus compared the reign of God to a tiny mustard seed which a man planted in his garden. This smallest of seeds grew into a large tree. In a twin parable, Jesus compared the reign of God to leaven which a woman mixed into a bushel of flour (Lk 13:18–21). The leaven grew and spread throughout the whole mass. The main point of both parables is that out of the smallest, most unlikely, even invisible beginnings, God can create something extremely valuable. In addition, by comparing the making of bread to his own mission of preaching the reign of God, Jesus gave great value to a task that his culture disparaged as woman's work.[21]

Jesus affirmed the presence and importance of women, as well as men, among his hearers. To illustrate the need for persistence in prayer, Jesus told two similar stories, one about a man and one about a woman. An unexpected guest arrived at a man's house. The man had nothing to feed his guest, so he knocked on a friend's door at midnight, asking to borrow bread. The friend told him to quit bothering him at such a late hour. But the man kept knocking and asking for bread. Finally, because of the man's insistent pleading, the friend got up and gave him food (Lk 11:5–10). Jesus told a parallel story about a woman who was a widow, one of the most powerless people in that society. This widow went to a judge to demand justice from an enemy who was perhaps trying to cheat her out of what little she had. Not from any belief in God or sense of justice, but because he got tired of the woman's persistent plea, the judge finally gave the widow her just rights (Lk 18:1–8). Jesus' point in both parables is that if imperfect human beings can be moved by pleas for justice, how much more will the just and righteous God respond to people's prayers for justice. Jesus' choice of a woman as the main character of one of these parables underscores this point. Through these parables, Jesus encourages women and men to pray and work for justice in an unjust system. He applauds perseverance in the woman as well as the man, even though his religious tradition often described persistence as a negative trait in a woman.[22]

In describing the end of the world, Jesus also used illustrations balancing female and male images. The Gospel of Matthew records Jesus' story of two men working out in the field; one would be taken and the other left. Likewise, two women would be grinding meal, and one would be taken and the other left (Mt 24:40–41). Luke's record of this story is slightly different: two men in bed parallel the two women grinding meal (Lk 17:34–35).

Jesus used another set of gender-balanced parables to reinforce his teaching concerning the end times. The parables of the faithful and unfaithful servants and the wise and foolish bridesmaids emphasized the impossibility of knowing when the final day will come and the need always to be prepared. The faithful servant carefully fulfilled the responsibilities the master gave him, and when the master returned, he found everything in order. The unfaithful servant beat his fellow servants and squandered his time in drunken orgies, thinking his master would not come and catch him. But the master came earlier than expected and caught the wicked servant

(Mt 24:45–51). In the parallel story the wise maidens took oil with their lamps when they went to meet the bridegroom. The foolish maidens took no oil with their lamps. The bridegroom arrived unexpectedly at midnight. The wise maidens went to the marriage feast with the bridegroom, while the foolish maidens had to go out and buy oil for their lamps. When they returned, it was too late (Mt 25:1–13). The structure of the parable of the maidens is almost exactly the same as the structure of the parable of the servants, again underscoring the equal value Jesus placed on women and men. Through male-female parallelism in these parables, Jesus shows that women and men can equally illustrate God's dealings with humankind.[23]

Jesus rejected the long-standing law that gave women harsher sentences for adultery than men (Num 5:11–31). No other religious leader of that time accused a man of committing adultery by divorcing his wife and marrying another woman (Mk 10:11). Jesus placed equal responsibility on the husband and wife for fidelity in marriage (Mk 10:2–12). He never warned men against the wiles of loose women, but against their own lust and aggression (Mt 5:27–28). Jesus placed responsibility for sexual aggression on the man, not on the woman who more often received blame in a male-oriented society. Unlike other religious leaders of his day, Jesus did not make women scapegoats in sexual matters (Jn 8:3–11). He rejected the double standard that placed more responsibility for sexual morality on women than on men.[24] Even today, society often blames a rape victim as somehow responsible for her rape through her seductive behavior. Jesus, on the other hand, espoused a feminist ethic of equal value and respect for women in sexual and familial relationships.

Jesus further demonstrated the value he placed on women by speaking of God as a woman. Jesus' portrayal of God as a woman shocked his hearers who did not think women worthy enough even to testify in a court of law or to control their own religious vows. Some people today still resist feminine references to God because of their lack of respect for the feminine. Jesus had no such sexist attitudes. He balanced the picture of God as a man in the parable of the lost sheep with the picture of God as a woman in the parable of the lost coin (Lk 15:3–10). In that parable Jesus taught that God is like a woman who had ten silver coins and lost one. Because the coin was so important to her, she searched diligently for it. When she finally found the lost coin, she called her friends and neighbors to rejoice with her. The main point of both the parable of the lost coin and the parable of the lost sheep is that God places great value on each individual.

In the parable of the lost coin, Jesus spoke of God as a woman. Referring to God as "She" today is not as radical as Jesus' feminine references to God in his own time and culture. Leonard Swidler comments on the negative attitude toward women throughout Christian history that kept theologians from a trinitarian interpretation of the three parables in Luke chapter 15. The parable of the prodigal son pictures God as Father; the parable of the lost sheep pictures God as the Good Shepherd, identified with Jesus; the parable of the lost coin pictures God as a woman, who should then logically be the Holy Spirit. Swidler explains that the failure to reach this logical trinitarian conclusion is not due to the Christian abhorrence of pagan goddesses leading to the rejection of a female image of God, because a similar Christian abhorrence of pagan gods would also have resulted in the rejection of a male image of God. Rather, the ignoring of Jesus' female image of God in this parable came from "an underlying widespread Christian deprecatory attitude toward women that blinded most Christian theologians and commentators to the strong feminism of Jesus in the Gospels."[25]

Jesus' feminism was so strong that he even used feminine images in self-references: "Jerusalem, Jerusalem, the city that kills the prophets and stones those who are sent to it! How often have I desired to gather your children together as a hen gathers her brood under her wings, and you were not willing!" (Mt 23:37). Jesus chose this maternal image to convey longing and unconditional love. Jesus used feminine traits to underscore this nurturing love. Another passage records Jesus' use of feminine imagery in an invitation to "come to me and drink" (Jn 7:37, RSV). The image of drinking from a human being could only be interpreted as a maternal image, but translations have rendered the Greek word *koilia* as "heart," when a more accurate translation would be "breast" (Jn 7:38). Biblical translators have been fearful of portraying Jesus as a mother inviting people to drink from her breasts, but Jesus had no such fears of femininity.[26]

JESUS' FEMINIST INCLUSIVENESS

If the Christ-event means anything for anyone, it means something for everyone. All christology begins and ends with a theological understanding of the God who is Creator and Sustainer becoming involved in human history for the salvation of humankind. Christology involves a "universal anthropological understanding of the human."[27] Jesus stands for each one of us in our human condition. The christological debates of the first five centuries assumed that the incarnation included all humankind, male and female. Incarnational doctrine emphasized God's taking on humanity, not maleness. The fourth-century Council of Nicea focused on Christ's becoming human, not becoming a male person. The Council of Chalcedon in the mid-fifth century declared Christ to be perfect in divinity and perfect in humanity, not perfect in maleness.[28] Theological tradition has almost always maintained that the maleness of Jesus is theologically, christologically, and sacramentally irrelevant.[29]

In his case for the ordination of women, Bill Leonard says that if women are too cursed to be ordained, they may be too cursed to be saved.[30] From this one might go on to say that if the feminine is too cursed to be included in the incarnation, then females are too cursed to be saved by Jesus. This is not a new idea but one that echoes the thought of a church father from the fourth century. Responding to the early heresy that Jesus was not fully human, Gregory of Nazianzus at the Council of Constantinople in 381 declared: "What has not been assumed cannot be restored; it is what is united with God that is saved."[31] If the feminine was not assumed in the incarnation of God in Jesus, then women cannot be redeemed.

Jesus assumed every aspect of humanity, feminine as well as masculine, Gentile as well as Jew. The maleness of the earthly Jesus, just like his Jewishness, has no ontological significance. When people identify Jesus with maleness, with Jewishness, or with first-century culture, they miss the point of Jesus' significance and mission. Jesus became flesh to show forth the love of God for all. Exalting the concrete details of Jesus' life in exclusively masculine representations misses the whole point of the incarnation and the nature of divine revelation. To exalt Jesus' maleness is to ignore central truths of the Christian tradition.[32] If Jesus is represented only in masculine images, consistency demands that Jesus also be represented only in Jewish images. The traditional church stands accused of failing to lift Jesus out of the particularity of gender. Artists have freely depicted Jesus as Gentile, but until recently have balked at feminine representations. It is clear that this bias does not come from the words and actions of Jesus, but from prejudice against women.

The Christian community of the first few centuries began to follow the actions of Jesus in opposition to cultural prejudices. Elisabeth Schüssler Fiorenza thoroughly demonstrates that the early Christian community was a "discipleship of equals."[33] When Constantine made Christianity the state religion, however, the church became a powerful support for the institutional sexism, racism, and imperialism of Roman society. "The Lordship of Christ ceased to liberate women, slaves, and conquered people from their lords and masters. Instead these lords and masters saw themselves as more 'like' Christ than their subjects and deriving their lordship from the Lordship of Christ."[34] Men in power used the image of Christ's Lordship as a divine sanction of their privileged positions.

Exclusively masculine references continue to hinder Jesus' message of good news for the poor and liberation for the oppressed (Lk 4:18). No matter how much we may emphasize Jesus' identification with women and with other oppressed people, masculine christological images sanction the status quo of men's holding the majority of power in church and society. The male image of Christ, no matter how closely associated with Jesus the liberator, continues to be used to exclude women and to sanction men in positions of power.

Language needs to reflect the human nature, rather than the male nature, of Jesus. Balancing feminine and masculine references to Jesus emphasizes the holistic human nature of Jesus. Expanding the Christian vocabulary to include "Christ-Sophia" and "She" goes a long way toward getting the complete message of Jesus across to all people. The first two chapters of this book have demonstrated that the designation "Christ-Sophia" has biblical and historical support. Through Christ-Sophia the prophetic message of Jesus can awaken today's church to the ministry of reconciliation and liberation.

It is a fact that the Christian tradition has over-emphasized masculine images of Christ to the detriment of both men and women. Men still bear a disproportionate burden of leadership in both church and society, and women still lack equal decision-making power and opportunities to develop fully their gifts. Adding "Christ-Sophia" and "She" to the language of Christian belief and worship brings home Jesus' message of good news for the poor and oppressed in a new and powerful way. These feminine references also serve as a vivid reminder to Christian men to model their lives on the feminist Jesus, who overcame the temptation to exercise male domination so that he might liberate and empower women and men, and enable them to work as equal partners toward the reign of God.

QUESTIONS FOR
REFLECTION AND DISCUSSION

1. Do you think the maleness of the historical Jesus has theological significance?

2. In what ways did Jesus challenge the male-dominated society in which he lived?

3. What feminist actions of Jesus would be considered revolutionary even today?

4. How do you think the Christian church would be different if it had taken as seriously Jesus' words concerning the woman who anointed him with perfume, "What she has done will be told in remembrance of her" (Mk 14:9), as it has taken Jesus' words at the last supper, "Do this in remembrance of me" (Lk 22:19)?

5. In what ways was Jesus' language radically inclusive in the context of first-century culture?

6. How is Jesus' language more inclusive than that of most Christians today?

7. How do exclusively masculine christological references hinder Jesus' message of liberation today?

8. How do you feel about pictures of Jesus as a blond, blue-eyed Gentile? as an African? as a woman? Do you believe there are theological differences in these three representations?

9. How do you feel when you call God "she"? When you call Christ "she"?

CHAPTER 4

The Risen
Christ-Sophia

The question most often raised when I am leading discussions on Christian feminism and inclusive language is, "You do believe Jesus is male, don't you?" The intent is to trap me into a literalistic either-or position. I do not deny the maleness of the historical Jesus. But if I answer in the affirmative, they quickly jump to what they see as the logical conclusion: Since Jesus is male, and since Jesus and God are one, then God is male. Instead of answering this question, I let them know that their question misses the point of Jesus altogether. I remind them of the discussion between Jesus and the Sadducees on the question of the resurrection.

A group of Sadducees, who did not believe in life after death, came to Jesus with some practical problems they had with the teaching about the resurrection. According to Mosaic levirate marriage law, the brother of a man who died without a son had an obligation to marry the widow (Dt 25:5–10). The Sadducees presented a hypothetical case to Jesus of a woman who, after her husband died childless, married his brother. Then that husband died childless, and she married another brother. This went on until she had married all seven brothers. Finally the woman died. The Sadducees, trying to discredit the doctrine of the resurrection, asked Jesus whose wife she would be in the resurrection. Jesus' answer went beyond such a literalistic viewpoint. He let them know that they had missed the point of the resurrection altogether. The resurrection transcends human concepts of marriage. In the resurrection there will be no marriage because all will be "like angels and are children of God, being children of the resurrection" (Lk 20:36).

Questions about Jesus' maleness are like the Sadducees' questions about whose wife the widow would be in the resurrection. They miss the point. Jesus clearly tells the Sadducees that the resurrection is a reality different from any they have known in "this age" (Lk 20:34). Human concepts of marriage and gender do not apply to the resurrection. In the same way the question of Jesus' maleness becomes totally irrelevant to an understanding of the resurrected Jesus.

The relegation of Jesus to the past presents a fundamental problem for Christianity. Churches often study the biblical materials on the life of the historical Jesus without applying the teachings and actions of Jesus to the current mission of the church. The Christian church has traditionally used belief in the resurrection as a test of orthodoxy while seldom searching for the relevance of the resurrection to the current life of the church. In similar fashion Christian communities regularly use language and actions in worship services that reinforce an image of the historical Jesus as interpreted by those in power in institutional Christianity. The Jesus who preached salvation to the powerless, the poor, and the oppressed has been overshadowed by representations of Jesus as sanctioning the institutional status quo. The church has often missed the point of the mission of the historical Jesus and the transforming power of the resurrection.

The challenge for Christianity today is to reclaim the centrality of the resurrection for the faith. But it is not enough to affirm belief in the resurrection. Resurrection faith must lead believers in search of the meaning the risen Christ-Sophia gives to life today. Resurrection faith should empower people for the ongoing mission of restoring human relationships, institutions, and the whole cosmos.

THE CENTRALITY OF THE RESURRECTION

The resurrection was central to the early church's missionary proclamation. The apostle Paul unequivocally stated the necessity of the resurrection to the Christian faith: "If Christ has not been raised, then our proclamation has been in vain and your faith has been in vain" (1 Cor 15:14). Paul believed that without the resurrection, the Christian faith was futile. Without the resurrection, there could be no Christianity.

The apostle Peter's earliest sermons center on the resurrection. At Pentecost, Peter proclaimed, "This Jesus God raised up, and of that all of us are witnesses" (Acts 2:32). After healing the crippled beggar at the Beautiful Gate, Peter witnessed to the power of the resurrection: "You killed the Author of life, whom God raised from the dead. To this we are witnesses" (Acts 3:15). Peter testified that faith in this resurrected One brought restored health to the crippled man.

In the early church, the resurrection constituted the core of the Christian proclamation. The resurrection formed the essence of the faith of the disciples and the faith of the church: "With great power the apostles gave their testimony to the resurrection of the Lord Jesus, and great grace was upon them all" (Acts 4:33). The resurrection became an inseparable part of the gospel. The early church proclaimed "a new birth into a living hope through the resurrection of Jesus Christ from the dead, and into an inheritance that is imperishable, undefiled, and unfading" (1 Pt 1:3–4).

The early followers of Jesus regarded the resurrection as fundamental to the existence of the new Christian movement. The primary duty of a disciple was to witness to belief in the resurrection. For the disciples, the validity of the resurrection rested on their personal experience, not on theological arguments.[1] If Jesus' disciples had not been certain of the resurrection, their faith in Jesus would not have survived their bewilderment and disappointment at the crucifixion.[2] The faith of the early church rested on transforming encounters with the risen One.

The apostle Paul proclaimed Jesus' resurrection and share in God's sovereign rule over the world as essential to the Christian faith. To the Athenians, Paul preached "the good news about Jesus and the resurrection" (Acts 17:18). In his writings Paul emphasized the basic gospel message concerning Jesus' death and resurrection and paid little attention to Jesus' mission in Galilee and Jerusalem. Paul did not speak very often of Jesus' earthly life, but instead focused on Christ's glory and power since the resurrection.[3] Paul declared the risen Christ to be "the power of God and the wisdom (*Sophia*) of God" (1 Cor 1:24). Knowledge of Christ-Sophia became inseparable from the resurrection; Paul longed "to know Christ and the power of [Christ's] resurrection" (Phil 3:10). There could be no knowledge of Christ or faith in Christ without the resurrection: "If Christ has not been raised, your faith is futile and you are still in your sins" (1 Cor 15:17).

If Christians do not take the step from the historical Jesus to the resurrected Christ-Sophia who still lives in the church and in the cosmos, then their worship of Jesus becomes meaningless. They could study the impact of the historical Jesus in various forms and find inspiration in Jesus as a model for behavior, much as people find inspiration in the life of Socrates.[4] But only faith in the risen One alive today can truly inspire Christian worship and mission. As Jürgen Moltmann states, "Christianity stands or falls with the reality of the raising of Jesus from the dead by God. In the New Testament there is no faith that does not start a priori with the resurrection of Jesus....A Christian faith that is not resurrection faith can therefore be called neither Christian nor faith."[5]

The Christian concept of God depends upon the resurrection. Faith in the resurrection is not a supplement to belief in God and in Jesus Christ; it is the essence of that belief.[6] Christian faith rests on belief in a God who cares enough about humankind and all of creation to become incarnate in the world. God understands the human condition and is actively engaged in bringing redemption to the world. "For we do not have a high priest who is unable to sympathize with our weaknesses, but we have one who in every respect has been tested as we are, yet without sin. Let us therefore approach the throne of grace with boldness, so that we may receive mercy and find grace to help in time of need" (Heb 4:15–16). This understanding, empathetic God could not be limited to the short span of the life of the historical Jesus. Because of the resurrection, this loving God still lives, providing continual access to grace. The significance of the resurrection to the Christian faith cannot be overestimated.

The resurrection gives Christianity its universal significance. It moves Christianity out of the past and into the present and the future. It lifts the incarnation out of the particularities of race, culture, and gender into a universal inclusiveness. The resurrection not only attests to the divinity of Jesus, but also to the continual relevance of the Christian faith. Because of the resurrection, Christ-Sophia continues to redeem human beings and all of creation.

Christ-Sophia lives as a gracious, transforming Spirit. She continues to become incarnate in the individual believer and in the church. The Christian faith is an incarnational faith, and the resurrection makes this faith possible. Believers incarnate the Spirit of Christ-Sophia: "It is no longer I who live, but it is Christ who lives in me" (Gal 2:20). The relationship between Jesus and the Spirit illustrates the centrality of the resurrection in earliest christological thought (Acts 1:8). Only with the resurrection did Jesus become the life-giving Spirit.

THE MEANING OF THE RESURRECTION

The New Testament writers thought of the risen Jesus in terms of the Spirit. The identification in the New Testament between Jesus and the Spirit begins with the resurrection. According to John's Gospel, the first sending of the Holy Spirit took place on Easter Day itself. After appearing to Mary Magdalene, the risen Jesus appeared to the other disciples and breathed on them, saying, "Receive the Holy Spirit" (Jn 20:22).

Paul equates the Spirit of God and the Spirit of the resurrected Christ: "But you are not in the flesh; you are in the Spirit, since the Spirit of God dwells in you. Anyone who does not have the Spirit of Christ does not belong to [Christ]. But if Christ is in you, though the body is dead because of sin, the Spirit is life because of righteousness" (Rom 8:9–10). Paul uses the terms "Spirit of God" and "Spirit of Christ" to indicate the risen One who dwells within believers. Paul makes no distinction between the believer's experience of the Spirit of the resurrected Christ and the Spirit of God. The experience of intimate union with the resurrected One comes through the Spirit. For Paul, the resurrected Christ can be experienced only in and through the Spirit.[7] The resurrection means that Christ-Sophia is alive today, still encountering believers through the Spirit and as the Spirit.

From the beginning the theology of the Christian movement identifies the resurrected One not only with the Spirit of God but also with the Sophia of God. In Hebrew and in Aramaic, both terms are grammatically feminine. Paul's argument in chapters 1 and 2 of First Corinthians evidences that the Christian missionary movement understood the resurrected Christ in terms of Sophia and Spirit. Apollos and some other early disciples, though baptized into John's baptism of repentance, had not heard of the Holy Spirit (Acts 18:24—19:6). The more accurate teaching of Priscilla and Aquilla focused on the gospel of the resurrected Christ, who is understood as life-giving Holy Spirit and Sophia. The content of the more accurate "Way of God," which Priscilla and Aquila explained to Apollos, may have been similar to the christological formula which calls the resurrected One "the power of God and the wisdom (*Sophia*) of God" (1 Cor 1:24).[8]

Because of the resurrection Christ-Sophia gives power and wisdom to believers through the Spirit. Because of the resurrection Christians have the gift of God's Spirit. The Spirit makes possible any meaningful statements believers can make about the resurrection. Schillebeeckx states that while the resurrection is a historical event, it is "per se trans-historical." He does not negate the historicity of the empty tomb and the resurrection appearances of Jesus, but states that "belief in the Jesus who is risen and lives with God and among us cannot be founded on an empty tomb" alone.[9] Faith in the resurrection comes from God's revelation and grace through the Spirit. Miriam Therese Winter asserts that the resurrection reminds us not to attribute traits of the historical Jesus to the risen Christ, "who transcends all limitations of gender, all limitations of culture, all limitations of flesh itself and, in a truly inclusive Spirit, continues to come again."[10]

The significance of the risen One lies not in visual appearance. The risen Christ-Sophia did not have the particular physical features of Jesus in the flesh. The disciples on the Emmaus road initially did not even recognize Jesus (Lk 24:13–35). The specific physical form of the historical Jesus, including gender and race, was not part of the essence of the resurrected Christ-Sophia. More important than the physical reality was the spiritual reality of the risen One. This spiritual reality established the disciples' faith.[11] Physical

form was not part of Paul's experience of the risen Savior on the
road to Damascus. Paul simply saw light and heard a voice (Acts
9:1–7). In his own account of this experience, Paul does not even
mention voices or visible light (Gal 1:12,15–17). When Paul speaks
of the resurrection, the emphasis falls rather on the power of Christ-
Sophia to give life filled with divine grace, forgiveness, and love.[12]

The resurrection does not mean the rising of Jesus into the old
life, but the beginning of the new creation. The resurrection is more
than a historical event; it is a "supra-historical" event beyond the
historian's purview. It belongs in the realm of faith.[13] Paul refuted
literalistic views of the resurrection: "But someone will ask, 'How
are the dead raised? With what kind of body do they come?' Fool!
What you sow does not come to life unless it dies. And as for what
you sow, you do not sow the body that is to be, but a bare seed, perhaps of wheat or of some other grain" (1 Cor 15:35–37). Paul was
convinced that the risen One who appeared to him belonged to another order of existence than the Jesus whom the disciples had
known in the flesh. An imperishable spiritual body had to replace
the perishable physical body (1 Cor 15:42–44). Resurrection thus results in a new creation, unlimited by time, culture, race, and gender.

One of the most recent developments in christology is toward
"Christ-ology," that is, a study of Jesus becoming the Christ
through the resurrection. From this perspective Christ-Sophia calls
a new creation into being through the resurrection, and only
through the resurrection does Jesus become the Messiah.[14] Through
the resurrection Jesus gains full possession of the Spirit and full saving power to transform human history. Viewed in this way
Christian soteriology cannot be limited to reflection about the person and activity of the historical Jesus. It must deal with the saving
action that began with Easter and that continues in the present and
into the future until the eschaton.[15]

Neil Lightfoot entitles his commentary on the Book of Hebrews,
Jesus Christ Today, because Hebrews emphasizes Christ-Sophia's activity for all ages. Hebrews goes beyond a first-century exhortation
to become a contemporary challenge. The writer of Hebrews urges
Christians then and now to pay attention to the Word that not only
spoke in the past but also speaks to the present.[16] The saving work
of Christ-Sophia continues the work begun by the historical Jesus.

Although Jesus' sacrificial death took place in history, it continues "for all time" (Heb 10:12). The phrase "once for all," repeated often in Hebrews, underscores the universality of the work of Christ-Sophia.[17]

The resurrection presents an altogether new possibility for the world, for human existence, and for history. The resurrection signifies that the reign of God which Jesus had announced and demonstrated did not die. The way of the cross becomes the way for God to reign on the earth. The Spirit of God who was in Jesus lives on in those who, no matter what the cost, practice the reign of God with all its implications of justice, liberty, truth, and peace. The resurrection means that the reign of God the Spirit can come to all. It makes available to all the gift of the Holy Spirit and symbolizes the democratization and inclusiveness of the gospel. Through the resurrection Christ-Sophia did not establish a priestly class to dispense salvation, but provided all people with direct access to God. The clergy hold no essential power as dispensers of divine grace; rather everyone depends on the Spirit for salvation.[18]

The resurrection transforms both individuals and the entire cosmos. It affirms the unity of matter and spirit, redeeming creation from domination and exploitation, and provides hope that things do not have to remain as they are. Pulling back the layers of Greek dualism reveals that this most basic of Christian beliefs supports ecological efforts to preserve and restore creation.[19] Thus resurrection christology rises above individual or even corporate human transformation to embrace all of creation.

Matthew Fox underscores this meaning of the resurrection as inclusive of all creation: "I believe the appropriate symbol of the Cosmic Christ who became incarnate in Jesus is that of Jesus as Mother Earth crucified yet rising daily....Mother Earth is being crucified in our time and is deeply wounded....Yet, like Jesus, she rises from her tomb every day."[20] Fox believes that symbolizing Jesus as Mother is biblical (Lk 13:34) and essential to transforming a patriarchal civilization bent on destroying the earth.

Christin Lore Weber also re-visions the death-resurrection mystery to include the feminine. Weber emphasizes the prominent part women play in the biblical resurrection story. In addition, Weber lifts Mary, the mother of Jesus, from her traditional subordinate role to that of equal partner with Jesus in redemption:

Contrary to androcentric interpretation, she [Mary] does not take her meaning from him; rather, she is a source of meaning in her self, as woman. She is, with him, the original priest: there can be no priesthood when they are separate, one from the other. She is ultimate. She contains the emptiness from which he springs forth. Out of her he lives, and into her he dies. Together they are the process of creation, the ebb and the flow.[21]

For Weber, Mary serves as a symbol of the archetypal woman joining with the archetypal man to transform creation: "Together they accepted death — the New Woman and the New Man — and it made them dangerous, powerful, the beginning of a new cycle of life."[22] While this understanding of Mary's role is thought-provoking, it lacks a strong biblical or traditional foundation and is open to critique. The image of Christ-Sophia provides a stronger symbol of the power of the male-female union to bring new life. It is also more central to biblical revelation about Christ and the power of the resurrection.

The resurrection overcomes alienation and promises healing and restoration to human beings and to the whole cosmos.

For the creation waits with eager longing for the revealing of the children of God; for the creation was subjected to futility, not of its own will but by the will of the one who subjected it, in hope that the creation itself will be set free from its bondage to decay and will obtain the freedom of the glory of the children of God. We know that the whole creation has been groaning in labor pains until now; and not only the creation, but we ourselves, who have the first fruits of the Spirit, groan inwardly while we wait for adoption, the redemption of our bodies. (Rom 8:19-23)

While the resurrection includes the whole of creation, traditional linguistic and visual symbols of the risen One have not reflected this inclusiveness. These traditional images, such as "King," "Lord," "Master," the "New Man," the "New Adam," and "He," bury the feminine, allowing only the masculine to rise to new life. Such images have never been psychologically satisfying because they represent only partial truth. The feminine image of the resurrected One, whether in the form of Jesus as Mother Earth or Mary or the Christ Mother of medieval Christian mystics, continually rises to consciousness.[23] Especially in times of crisis or illness, people cry out for comfort to Mary or to a mother-figure. Carl Jung interpreted Pope Pius XII's declaration of the Assumption of Mary as foretelling a world consciousness of the archetypal feminine rising after centuries of being buried by androcentric power and authority.[24] The feminine takes on power and rises to new life in the symbol of Christ-Sophia.

The resurrection means that Christ-Sophia continues the process of "making all things new" (Rev 21:5). Resurrection puts faith more in the present and future tenses than in the past tense. The resurrected Christ-Sophia opens new possibilities for language and action, worship and mission. The resurrection brings hope of overcoming alienation between male and female, matter and spirit, human and non-human creation. It also makes possible the restoration of relationships among the races and the elimination of all forms of oppression. In a world shaking on the brink of economic and ecological destruction, the resurrection promises new life. The risen Christ-Sophia lives as a witness to new creation and as the empowering Spirit who makes possible this new creation. Christ-Sophia lives today as the "power of God and the wisdom of God" (1 Cor 1:24), available to all who participate in "making all things new."

THE MISSION OF THE RESURRECTION

Christ-Sophia sends believers on a mission to make the resurrection a continual reality. The importance of the resurrection in history is that it provides hope and power for the mission of the church today. Resurrection theology inspires believers to resurrection living. Because of the resurrection, believers cannot be satisfied with the way things are. Christians are constantly challenged toward the vision of new life: "So if anyone is in Christ, there is a new creation: everything old has passed away; see, everything has become new!" (2 Cor 5:17).

The first followers of the risen Christ-Sophia acted on this vision.

They changed their lifestyles to follow Jesus in bringing good news to the poor and freedom to the oppressed (Lk 4:18). The resurrection gave them wisdom and grace to redistribute their wealth so that everyone had enough: "There was not a needy person among them, for as many as owned lands or houses sold them and brought the proceeds of what was sold" (Acts 4:34). The resurrection led the early Christians to transform economic inequities, breaking down divisions between rich and poor so that everyone was free to become all that God created them to be.

The resurrected Christ-Sophia calls today's Christians to continue that mission of liberation. This reality begins as people claim the freedom to grow into the divine image according to which God created them. They no longer have to live under the old ways of gender, race, and class oppression. There is no more subordination of Greek to Jew, slave to free, female to male; for all are equal in Christ-Sophia (Gal 3:28). Although hierarchies and oppression still exist, Christ-Sophia frees people to move toward the new creation. Even though most institutions, including churches, still function in a patriarchal mode, the risen Christ-Sophia offers a freedom that allows people to envision the new creation and to act to make this vision a reality in even the most stifling of institutions. Christ-Sophia empowers people to think and speak of the new creation so that it can become a reality within them. Whether they choose to stay in traditional churches and change the words of liturgies and the common meaning of symbols, or whether they form new faith communities committed to inclusive language and leadership, they are choosing freedom and growth toward the divine image of Christ-Sophia.

Claiming internal freedom empowers people to assist in liberating others. The resurrection brings hope of the fulfillment and wholeness of humankind as it continues the process of redemption, justice, peace, forgiveness, and liberation. The resurrection actualizes Christian freedom.[25] Confident of the liberating power of the resurrection, Christians can participate with Christ-Sophia in breaking down all forms of oppression that stand as barriers to this freedom. The resurrection provides a sign of God's restoration of humanity and of the power of love to bring new life.

The resurrection also affirms the unity within diversity of the human race. The risen One, unlimited by the particularities of the historical Jesus, furthers the dream of inclusiveness by including females and males of all races in the process of salvation and liberation. The risen Christ-Sophia symbolizes differences while making possible universal reconciliation.

The mission of the resurrection includes the freeing not only of humankind but of all God's creation. The resurrection begins the triumph for all humankind and for the entire cosmos over the forces of oppression and alienation. The risen Christ-Sophia sends all people on a mission to reconcile the whole world and heal the divisions produced by hierarchical systems, in order to preserve the purpose of all beings and nurture the interconnectedness of the world. In this way the resurrection undergirds all ecological efforts to conserve the earth and its creatures.

Belief in the resurrection provides confidence in a potential far beyond existing reality — a confidence in the triumph of life over death. Easter faith sends believers on a mission to discover creative potentialities. The resurrection opens the world to the future. It promises not just a repetition of history, but a continual creation of the new. The resurrection begins with the historical Jesus and continues with the cosmic Christ-Sophia redeeming all creation. Just as the Spirit "in the beginning" hovered over the waters to give birth to the universe and just as the Spirit raised Jesus from the dead, so the Spirit of Christ-Sophia continues to bring forth new life.

The image of Christ-Sophia awakens the imagination to the continual birthing that takes place through creation and resurrection. A christology centered on the resurrection maintains a continual openness to creative possibilities. It inspires hope that the feminine dimension of the divine, killed by patriarchy, can rise again to bring new power and wisdom. It taps human creativity so that people become co-creators with Christ-Sophia. Such a christology naturally leads to new linguistic formulations, such as Christ-Sophia, to express the theology of the all-inclusiveness of the risen One.

Resurrection christology makes universal claims that demand consideration in the light of the human needs and social problems of today. The church's mission begins with the question: Where and how do we meet the resurrected Christ-Sophia today? Unless we find Christ-Sophia alive in the world today, then our faith is in vain. Unless resurrection theology inspires resurrection actions that apply to current human needs and social problems, then faith is dead.

Christ-Sophia gives rise to a living faith. Walking hand-in-hand with Christ-Sophia, we continually discover the meaning of the resurrection for each time and place. Christ-Sophia frees us from narrow ways of thinking and challenges us to new ideas and new ways of being. Through the indwelling Spirit of Christ-Sophia we receive power to make the vision of the new creation a reality. In this way we open ourselves to new and creative possibilities as we continue in search of the resurrected Christ-Sophia.

QUESTIONS FOR
REFLECTION AND DISCUSSION

1. How is the question concerning the maleness of Jesus irrelevant to the resurrected Jesus?

2. What do you believe to be the significance of the resurrection to Christian theology?

3. Do you connect belief in the risen Jesus with belief in the Holy Spirit?

4. How do you picture the historical Jesus? How do you picture the risen Jesus?

5. What meanings does the resurrection have for you?

6. How does the name "Christ-Sophia" expand the meaning of the resurrection?

7. What do you believe to be the mission of the Christian church today? In what ways does the image of the resurrected Christ-Sophia contribute to this mission?

PART II

Claiming the Power of the Resurrected Christ-Sophia

CHAPTER 5

CHRIST-SOPHIA SPIRITUALITY

"Christ [-Sophia] in you, the hope of glory." (Colossians 1:27)

The search for Christ-Sophia acting in the world today involves not only the theological question of who God is, but the existential question of who we are. Our confessions of faith reveal ourselves, since they are limited by our theological understanding and experience. The historical reality of Jesus finds meaning only in the here and now of our present reality.[1] The search for the resurrected Christ-Sophia then becomes not only the search for ultimate reality, but also the search for authentic personhood.

Paul speaks of Christ-Sophia living within him: "I have been crucified with Christ; and it is no longer I who live, but it is Christ who lives in me" (Gal 2:19–20). Writing to the Christians at Galatia, Paul pictures himself as a mother "in the pain of childbirth until Christ is formed" in those who hear his message (Gal 4:19). Paul goes on to say that "as many of you as were baptized into Christ have clothed yourselves with Christ" (Gal 3:27). Despite the fact that some Christian traditions overemphasize individual salvation, the Christian faith nonetheless speaks to the transformation of individuals as well as societies. In this context the search for the resurrected Christ-Sophia leads inward as well as outward.

The Book of Hebrews emphasizes the meaning of Christ-Sophia for today and "for all time" (Heb 10:12). Christ-Sophia fulfills the prophet Jeremiah's vision of a new covenant. Through Christ-Sophia, God offers us a covenant not based on external laws, but on internal spiritual power: "I will put my laws in their minds, and write them on their hearts, and I will be their God, and they shall be my people....For I will be merciful toward their iniquities, and I will remember their sins no more" (Heb 8:10,12). This new covenant releases us from rigid rules and roles and from the stranglehold of sin and guilt, so that we become free to search for the risen Christ-Sophia within ourselves.

The new covenant invites all people to this search: "They shall all know me, from the least of them to the greatest" (Heb 8:11). With the new covenant the knowledge of divine matters is not the private possession of a particular class or race or gender. No longer can there be distinctions between laity and clergy. Knowledge of God is accessible to all alike: "There is no longer Jew or Greek, there is no longer slave or free, there is no longer male and female; for all of you are one in Christ Jesus" (Gal 3:28). The picture of Christ-Sophia brings these foundational biblical truths into clearer focus. The name "Christ-Sophia" implies in new and powerful ways the equal inclusion of male and female, Jew and Greek.

As we free the Christ-Sophia within us, we feel included in God's love and included in the faith community. The freedom we have in Christ-Sophia is the freedom whose ultimate foundation is the liberating love of God (Gal 2:4).[2] This freedom involves love of ourselves, others, and God. Christ-Sophia frees us from that within ourselves that keeps us from loving ourselves and from loving God and others. The freedom we have in Christ-Sophia is the freedom to become all God created us to be. It enables us to find healing of our wounds and liberation from stereotypes and prescribed roles. Our search leads to our own resurrection while affirming the resurrection of Christ-Sophia. In this way Christ-Sophia provides a model of resurrection not only from physical death, but also from dead tradition.

NEW WAYS OF INTERPRETING SCRIPTURE

The basic principles of Christ-Sophia spirituality proceed naturally to an interpretation of scripture and tradition in ways that overcome oppression and foster liberation. Feminist theologians of the past few decades are not the first to recognize the social and political power of scripture. In 1895, Elizabeth Cady Stanton published *The Woman's Bible*, analyzing passages referring to women according to whether they oppress or liberate women. Although Stanton's work lacks theological sophistication and is marred by inaccuracies, it nevertheless reveals a woman living a century ago who listened to her own inner wisdom. This wisdom led her to biblical passages that teach "love, charity, liberty, justice and equality for all the human family."[3]

Shortly before the people of Israel entered the promised land, Moses issued an invitation to them: "I call heaven and earth to witness against you today that I have set before you life and death, blessings and curses. Choose life so that you and your descendants may live" (Dt 30:19). Moses challenged the people to see that the promised land was more than a physical place of security and safety and prosperity. The promised land was a spiritual choice they must continually make. This ancient wisdom can inform us today as we make our exodus from traditional interpretations that stifle human gifts and limit divine truth. In the interpretation and application of scripture and tradition, Christ-Sophia leads us to reject that which brings death and curses and to choose that which brings life and blessings.

Feminist theologians use various designations for this type of liberating biblical interpretation. Elisabeth Schüssler Fiorenza develops a "feminist critical hermeneutics of the Bible," which integrates egalitarian traditions and texts into a reconstruction of scriptural theology and history. In her interpretation of scripture, Fiorenza chooses to focus on those remnants that reveal that patriarchy is not inherent in Christian revelation and community.[4] Rosemary Radford Ruether employs "biblical prophetic criticism" as a way of protesting the established order and of pointing toward new possibilities through the transformation of values.[5] I propose a "resurrection interpretation of the Bible," which brings new life through liberation from patriarchy. This resurrection hermeneutics of scripture brings freedom from oppressive interpretations and emphasizes that which is life-giving and life-renewing in scripture. Christ-Sophia inspires such interpretation because it includes both resurrection and wisdom theology. The Spirit of Christ-Sophia dwelling within each of us grants wisdom to interpret scripture so as to bring new life.

Many of today's adult Christians grew up receiving contradictory messages about God and about the roles of women and men. On the one hand, God was spoken of as being exclusively male, and only men held important leadership roles in the church. At the same time there was a strong message that all baptized believers should listen to the voice of God within and share in the priesthood of all the faithful. Even though I saw a priesthood of only male believers in the practice of my church, I was convinced that the priesthood of believers included me.

Many years before feminist theology awakened my consciousness with its new insights and possibilities, I learned to apply the doctrine of the priesthood of all believers to some situations that felt oppressive to me. Shortly after I became a mother, for example, I realized that Mother's Day sermons made me feel guilty and inadequate instead of blessed and affirmed. I heard sermon after sermon admonishing mothers to be self-sacrificing, patient, self-effacing, all-loving, and all-giving. The portrait preachers painted of the ideal mother seemed impossible for me to reach. They cited biblical passages, such as Proverbs chapter 31, and interpreted them in such a way as to make the godly mother appear tireless in her giving, working day and night to meet the needs of her family. Deep within my spirit, this interpretation struck a discord. It did not ring true to my experience of mothers and of mothering nor to my interpretation of scripture. When I listened to such sermons, I felt hopeless and powerless. So I chose to protect my spirit by staying away from church on Mother's Day or by substituting my own interpretation for that of the preacher.

These Mother's Day sermons held up an ideal of motherhood impossible for any mortal mother to achieve. Only the Divine Mother could fulfill such an ideal. But the church did not give me a picture of the Divine Mother in scripture. No one ever taught me that the first picture of God in the Bible is that of a Mother giving birth to the universe, and that the Spirit who moved over the "face of the waters" to give birth to all life is the feminine *ruah*.[6] A picture of the Divine Mother might have erased the impossible ideal of human motherhood, and encouraged me to draw strength from this Mother who had created me in her image. This Divine Mother could also have kept me from feeling that I had to do everything, because she could take over when I felt weak and inadequate and limited.

The theological understanding of Christ-Sophia expands the importance of and gives greater validity to the feminine images throughout the Bible. Christ-Sophia empowers us to listen to the voice of wisdom within us when we are reading scripture and participating in worship services. The image of Christ-Sophia helps us to believe on the deepest level that we are created in the divine image. In the image of Christ-Sophia, we can believe that Divine Wisdom lives in us. We can trust the voice of wisdom within us and truly believe that we share fully in the priesthood of Jesus Christ. Thus we interpret scripture and worship traditions through the Wisdom of Christ-Sophia, rejecting that which quenches the Spirit and choosing that which brings new life and blessing.

NEW WAYS OF PRAYING

The image of Christ-Sophia also inspires new ways of praying. When we pray to Christ-Sophia, we are praying for new possibilities and new directions. We open ourselves to uncharted paths and unexpected wisdom. Such praying requires vulnerability of spirit and deep faith in our connection with Divine Wisdom.

Mystics down through the centuries testify to the unknowableness of the divine and to the necessity of releasing ourselves into Divine Goodness as we pray. Saint Teresa of Avila prayed:

But alas, alas, my Creator, great anguish makes me utter complaints and speak of that for which there is no remedy until thou be pleased to send one. My imprisoned soul desires its freedom yet desires also not to swerve in the smallest degree from Thy Will....Why do I wish to weary myself by begging Thee for things fashioned by my desire, since Thou already knowest what are the ends of all that my understanding can conceive and my will desire, while I myself know not what is best for me? The very thing in which my soul thinks to find profit will perchance bring about my ruin.[7]

In this prayer St. Teresa agonizes as she tries to experience freedom of soul and at the same time pray according to God's will. She feels "great anguish" as she struggles between her desire for freedom and her desire for God's will. She suggests a resolution when she expresses trust in her Creator to understand and fulfill her deepest desires.

Praying to Christ-Sophia offers new possibilities of resolving the conflicts we feel when we try to pray by freely expressing our own desires while at the same time praying for God's will to be done. When Jesus taught his disciples to pray, "your will be done, on earth as it is in heaven" (Mt 6:10), he challenged them to pray that God's perfect reign of peace and justice be established on earth. However, "thy will be done" has come to be used with passive, fatalistic overtones. Often patients with a diagnosis of cancer use this phrase with a tone of resignation; it can become a hindrance to their fighting the disease. The phrase "thy will be done" forms a block to praying in that it suggests complete submission that flies in the face of beliefs concerning freedom of soul. It implies surrender to some implacable force above and beyond, over which a person has no control.

Christ-Sophia has opened up a new way of praying that holds freedom of soul and trust in God's purpose in tension. Instead of praying "thy will be done," we can pray "thy wisdom be done." If we pray in this way, we can believe that what comes is according to a deeper wisdom not out there or up there, but within our very being. Sometimes we may discover that we have prayed for something that we really did not desire deep within. We can trust the Wisdom of God to reveal our deepest desires through prayer and to fulfill them. We can trust the Spirit of Christ-Sophia to pray within us when we cannot even articulate our feelings and desires: "Likewise the Spirit helps us in our weakness; for we do not know how to pray as we ought, but that very Spirit intercedes with sighs too deep for words" (Rom 8:26).

Praying through Christ-Sophia thus changes the direction of our prayers. We do not pray to a God somewhere up there who is hard to reach. Rather, praying through Christ-Sophia puts us in touch with the Spirit of resurrection and wisdom within us. We can feel confidence and assurance that our prayers through Christ-Sophia will bring results according to the deepest wisdom within us. Thus our spirit finds freedom and new life through release to the kindly wisdom of Christ-Sophia.

Praying to Christ-Sophia involves confession and repentance of all that stifles resurrection and wisdom within us. Praying for forgiveness presents problems to many Christians, especially those steeped in guilt-inducing traditions and those women who too quickly blame themselves for not doing enough at home and at work. Ruth Duck points out that many traditional prayers of confession are inadequate in their delineation of sin. Such prayers often identify selfishness as sin, while admonishing self-sacrifice. While some need to confess the sin of selfishness, others need to confess the sins of self-doubt and self-effacement. Confession of selfishness undermines those women and men who need to grow in self-nurture and self-esteem.[8]

With these needs in mind I wrote a confessional prayer for the closing worship service of a "Woman as Healer" conference for health care professionals. At first I resisted having such a prayer in this service. But a colleague convinced me that if we were going to name ways in which we had been sinned against and stifled as healers, we also needed to name ways in which we had participated in this oppression, so that we might claim freedom. The following responsive prayer is an acknowledgment of our sins of self-doubt and self-negation and a claiming of power for change:

Leader: We have not trusted our deepest yearnings.

Circle 1:   Now Faith revives us to fulfill our inmost call.

Leader: We have not embraced the bounty of our bodies.

Circle 2:   Now Beauty beckons us to cherish and nourish ourselves.

Leader: We have not proclaimed the visions of our spirits.

Circle 3:   Now Hope inspires us to birth our dreams.

Leader: We have not developed the full potential of our minds.

Circle 1:   Now Wisdom enlightens us to become creators of a new world.

Leader: We have not claimed the fullness and diversity of our talents.

Circle 2:   Now Love empowers us to celebrate and nurture all our gifts.

Leader: We have not asserted our power and freedom as healers.

Circle 3:   Now truth sets us free to lead the way to wholeness.

All: Giver of all good gifts,
Revive us with your Faith,
Nourish us with your Beauty,
Inspire us with your Hope,
Enlighten us with your Wisdom,
Empower us with your Love,
Lead us by your Truth to become the
Healers you created us to be. Amen.

Praying to Christ-Sophia involves recognizing resistance both in ourselves and others. Many people are more comfortable talking about feminine images of God than using them in prayer and worship. They want to keep feminist theology in the realm of the academic and intellectual, feeling deeply threatened when someone suggests using feminine images for the divine in worship services. For example, some women on the planning committee of the "Woman as Healer" conference had no problem with a presentation on empowering feminine images of God in scripture, but they raised loud objections to the inclusion of these images in the closing worship service. They seemed especially threatened by references to Sophia in prayers and readings, even though Sophia is a biblical name for God. After many years of writing and speaking on feminine images of God, I still find it easier to talk about Christ-Sophia than to pray to her. Praying through Christ-Sophia invites and challenges us all to go beyond the intellectual level to the deepest feelings instilled in us since birth.

The resistance to praying in the name of Christ-Sophia stems from our socialization in a society in which male categories are normative and superior. One woman who was sincerely trying to apply her new insights about feminine images of God to her prayer life said, "It's so hard for me to call God 'She' or 'Mother,' because when I do, I don't feel that I'm giving God enough respect." This woman's statement reveals how thoroughly she has internalized her feelings of feminine inferiority. Baptist pastor Paul Smith partially explains this woman's feelings when he says that "the pervasive and sometimes subtle attitude that what is feminine is somehow inferior and evil—an integral part of our religious and cultural history—makes referring to God as female or feminine seem like we are accusing God of something bad."[9]

Although long ago we may have rejected such an attitude on a conscious level, seeds from this heritage lie within our unconscious minds. One of the major theologians of the Middle Ages, St. Anselm of Canterbury, states that calling God by feminine names is biblical. Since the Bible refers to God and Christ as Truth and Wisdom, both feminine nouns, Anselm believes we could call them Mother and Daughter. He states, however, that it is more appropriate to refer to them as Father and Son because it is "a natural fact in most instances," that the male is the superior sex.[10] Although most people today would reject Anselm's reason for referring to God in masculine terms, they nevertheless hold on to these terms, regardless of biblical evidence. Negative attitudes toward women imbedded in our religious tradition continue to influence us, whether or not we are aware of their power.

Our attachment to the familiar and comfortable also keeps us from praying through Christ-Sophia. With change occurring so rapidly in our world, we often hold on to religious traditions as the one area of stability in our lives. Even though these traditions may no longer meet our needs and in some cases may even cause pain, we often prefer to maintain them rather than risking the new and unknown in our spiritual lives. At times our need for safety and security is so great that we hold on to familiar behaviors even when they are painful and destructive.

Plato's "Allegory of the Cave" can highlight the struggles of modern believers clinging to deficient images of God. In this story a group of prisoners are chained deep within a dark cave. Since childhood they have been chained so that they can look only at the wall directly in front of them. Above and behind them a fire blazes. Between the fire and the prisoners there is a ledge on which people are walking back and forth, carrying on their daily activities. The prisoners see the shadows of these people on the wall before them. The shadows on the wall are the only reality the prisoners have ever known. Then one day someone comes down into the cave, releases several of the prisoners, and compels them to turn around so that they can see the reality behind the shadows. At first the light from the flame causes intense pain, and they find it unbearable to look at the real figures whose shadows they were used to seeing. At first they think the shadows are truer than the reality before them. They yearn to go back to the familiarity and comfort of their chained position. But their rescuer gradually leads them to face reality in the cave and then to move upward toward the greater light in the world outside the cave.

When they first emerge from the cave, their eyes are blinded by the light of the sun. They want to go back down into the cave to escape the pain the light causes. But gradually they open their eyes and begin to look around. Before long they are basking in the sunlight and running freely through fields of lush green and purple and rose. How could they have ever preferred the dark shadows of the cave to this glorious light and color and freedom? At last they realize that the freedom they are enjoying in the light was worth all the pain of the initial adjustment period.[11]

When we experience the light and new life that Christ-Sophia brings, we know that the change was worth all the pain and effort. Christ-Sophia frees us to pray, repenting of the ways that we have diminished ourselves and all creation, and claiming the power of wisdom within and around us. Christ-Sophia invites us to resurrected life as we connect with this Wisdom and trust ourselves to her goodness.

NEW AND FULLER CREATIVITY

Continuing our spiritual journey of connecting with Christ-Sophia, we can discover deep wells of creativity within ourselves. Just as Christ-Sophia was active in creation from the beginning, she continues to play a vital role in the creative process. She constantly "makes all things new" (Wis 7:27, Rev 21:5). Christ-Sophia invites everyone to join this perpetual dance of creativity. Believing we are truly in the image of the Divine Creator empowers us to embrace our creativity.

The inclusion of female and male in the naming of the Creator opens new creative possibilities for all people. In new and powerful ways, Christ-Sophia brings home the truth that we are all created in the image of God. Exclusively masculine images of God give women and men the subtle message that masculinity comes closer to the divine image. Women may try to minimize their femininity to come closer to the ideal or may come to distrust their creative gifts. Men may have trouble embracing aspects of their creativity that have been traditionally labeled and disparaged as feminine.

Christ-Sophia frees us all to open ourselves to the fullness and freedom of the creative Spirit within us. Christ-Sophia invites us to a wild abandonment as we create, and to a release of rigid stereotypes and prescribed structures. The very name of Christ-Sophia surprises us with freshness, beckoning us to venture along new paths.

Jesus and Sophia are both depicted in scripture as playful in their creativity. Jesus often used joking hyperbole to make a point: "It is easier for a camel to go through the eye of a needle than for someone who is rich to enter the kingdom of God" (Mk 10:25). Proverbs depicts Sophia as playfully adventurous in the creation of the universe. As Co-Creator with God, Sophia was "ever at play in God's presence" (Prv 8:30, Jerusalem Bible). Creation could not happen without Sophia's playful presence. Creativity needs an attitude of play.[12]

Matthew Fox, through his metaphor of the Cosmic Christ, also invites playful discovery of our creative gifts:

> The Cosmic Christ challenges us to embrace our powers of creativity: "Do not hide your light, your divine creative powers, under a bushel and thus allow human creativity to be manipulated and misused by forces of war making, destruction, pessimism, and bureaucracy. Find the creative person, the 'I am,' the divine child at play and at generativity in yourself. Give birth to yourself—your lifestyles, your relationships, your learning, your sexuality, your joys, your healing, your work—and build up in one another this same courage to create.... Come, play with me. Let us create together."[13]

Our creativity, like other aspects of spirituality, comes alive as we suspend rigid adult judgments and become playful, trusting children. Perhaps this is part of what Jesus meant when he said, "Unless you change and become like children, you will never enter the kingdom of heaven" (Mt 18:3). When we trust the creative Spirit within us, we come to feel the creative process as fun to be enjoyed instead of work to be accomplished.

As we experience the resurrrection of our childlike creativity amid our spirituality, we progress in faith and hope. But creativity in prayer or ministry or any other aspect of life does not happen automatically or easily. We may go through periods of waiting for something to happen. Perhaps we have an idea that we cannot quite bring to reality or a task we seem unable to accomplish. We struggle to create, but nothing comes. And we wait. Or we pray and pray about a situation, and we see nothing changing. We have to wait, holding on to hope. We wait believing that the Spirit of Christ-Sophia is at work within us. We wait with faith that there is a creative, spiritual power working according to Wisdom's timing, not our own. We wait then with confidence: "Now faith is the assurance of things hoped for, the conviction of things not seen" (Heb 11:1). We wait with hope and faith that something is happening, even though we cannot see it.

The creative process often feels like prayer. My deepest feelings of connection with Christ-Sophia often come when I am creating.

When I am writing, unplanned ideas and directions often come. In the process I feel like a co-creator with Christ-Sophia. But there are other times when I feel dry and blank. During these times I have to hold on to my faith so that seeds of creativity and spirituality which lie dormant will blossom again. Clarissa Pinola Estes believes that when the river of creativity disappears underground for a time, something is still developing. This is a natural part of a healthy creative life. But she cautions us not to dull the pain of waiting by filling the gaps with constant activity. In order to keep over-responsibility from stealing our necessary creative rests, we must learn to say "no."[14]

Women especially have trouble saying "no." We have been taught to take care of people and to be agreeable and sweet. Our inability to say "no" often keeps us from taking time to nurture our creative spirits. We have said "yes" to other voices for so long that we have silenced our own creative voices. One of the most powerful and memorable rituals at a national meeting of Women-Church began with worship leaders weaving in and out of circles beating drums.[15] As the drum beat grew louder and steadier, they began to chant a single word, "NO!" They invited all those gathered in that huge room to chant along with them. First softly and with some hesitation, the women began to chant, "No." I felt a little timid and uncomfortable as I joined the chant. Gradually the voices grew louder. The "No" swelled, reverberating throughout the room until it reached a shout. To my amazement, I could hear myself getting louder and louder, feeling more and more powerful as I chanted the word "No."

We must learn to say "no" so that we can say "yes" to our most creative and spiritual selves. We often have to go through a long period of negation before we reach the creative reservoirs within. Although this is a necessary period in the spiritual life, it may feel like walking through a dark, empty space. We search for Christ-Sophia, crying out with Job, "Where shall Wisdom be found? And where is the place of understanding? It is hidden from the eyes of all living" (Jb 28:12,21). Jazz musician and composer Benny Golson says that "the creative person always walks two steps into the darkness." The darkness is where "new things are discovered."[16]

Christ-Sophia spirituality leads us to risk walking into the unknown in order to make new discoveries. Even as we begin to use this new name for divinity, we open new possibilities. We come to greater realization of the power of naming in our faith development. As we overcome layers of resistance to the unfamiliar, we will be surprised by new insights. Praying to Christ-Sophia, reading scripture through the wisdom of Christ-Sophia, and creating by the inspiration of Christ-Sophia will bring new revelations beyond anything we currently imagine. We will come to a fuller understanding of who we are and experience a greater freedom to fulfill our potential in the divine image. We will experience resurrection as we become more closely connected with the Spirit of the resurrected Christ-Sophia dwelling within us. This resurrection is not a one-time, static event; rather it is a continual, dynamic process. Christ-Sophia invites us to constant seeking and discovery of new life. Our search continues.

QUESTIONS FOR
REFLECTION AND DISCUSSION

1. How would a theology based on the image of Christ-Sophia be freeing for you?

2. Have you heard interpretations of scripture passages that felt oppressive to you? How would you apply a "resurrection interpretation" to these passages?

3. Does praying "Thy Wisdom be done" feel any different to you than praying "Thy will be done"?

4. How do you feel when you pray to Christ-Sophia? In what ways do your prayers change?

5. How do you feel when you talk about feminine images of God in scripture? How do you feel when you use feminine names for God in private and public worship?

6. Does the inclusion of female and male in naming the Creator open new creative possibilities for you?

7. How might Christ-Sophia spirituality lead you to new creative discoveries? What other divine images spark your creativity?

CHAPTER 6

Christ-Sophia and Social Justice

"As you did it to one of the least of these . . . you did it to me."
(Matthew 25:40)

The search for the resurrected Christ-Sophia leads us from the personal freedom of Christ-Sophia dwelling within us to the freedom of serving with our hurting sisters and brothers. Jesus' words guide our search: "I was hungry and you gave me food, I was thirsty and you gave me something to drink, I was a stranger and you welcomed me, I was naked and you gave me clothing, I was sick and you took care of me, I was in prison and you visited me....Truly I tell you, just as you did it to one of the least of these who are members of my family, you did it to me" (Mt 25:35-36,40). In this parable of the last judgment, Jesus does not say a word about correct doctrine, but only about acting to meet the most ordinary human needs.[1] He identifies with those in need to the point that ministering to them is ministering to Jesus. This means that Christ-Sophia can be found as we serve with our sisters and brothers in need.

Christ-Sophia inspires ministry integrally connected with social justice. Reflection on the gospel leads to engagement in social struggle.[2] In her book, *Co-Creating: A Feminist Vision of Ministry*, Lynn Rhodes emphasizes that solidarity with those in need forms the basis for ministry. She says that ministry is not something we do "for others, but with others in the mutual struggle for new life."[3]

Working in solidarity with the poor and oppressed reveals the interconnectedness of all life. Jesus acted out the message that the power to change the world comes from solidarity with the oppressed.[4] Those who give also receive, and those who receive also give. The givers need the receivers just as much as the receivers need the givers. In *Strength to Love*, Martin Luther King, Jr., states that all of us "are caught in an inescapable network of mutuality, tied in a single garment of destiny. Whatever affects one directly, affects all indirectly. I can never be what I ought to be until you are what you ought to be, and you can never be what you ought to be until I am what I ought to be."[5]

This mutuality is seen in an incident from the ministry of a hospital chaplain intern named Julia who took the pediatrics unit as part of her assignment.[6] One afternoon as she was visiting children and their parents, Julia found a three-year-old girl named Angela alone in her room. As she approached Angela, Julia was struck with pity. The little girl's body was twisted and deformed, her head jerked back by the severe curvature of her spine. Angela was softly whimpering as she struggled to breathe. Julia began to stroke Angela and to talk softly to her. Angela quit crying and went to sleep. Julia learned that Angela had been born with cerebral palsy. Her mother struggled to support Angela and four other children with two jobs that paid only minimum wages. Other relatives tried to do what they could to help supplement their meager financial resources. Rarely did anyone come to stay with Angela in the hospital.

Julia determined to spend as much time with Angela as possible, because she was truly one of the "least of these." Every day for several weeks Julia visited Angela, with mixed feelings of duty, sympathy, and dread. Angela forced Julia to face some troubling theological questions. Why did Angela come into the world with so much against her? Where was God for Angela? Why do innocent children have to suffer?

One day these questions lost their urgency for Julia. As she looked into Angela's eyes, Julia saw for the first time a deep peace and joy. As their eyes truly met, Julia felt a profound connection with Angela. She felt the peace and joy she saw in Angela's eyes. For a moment there was recognition. As she gazed into the eyes of Angela, she knew she was looking into the eyes of Christ-Sophia.

From that day on, Julia went to Angela's room to receive as well as to give. Angela became Christ-Sophia to Julia, just as Julia was Christ-Sophia to Angela.

MINISTRY THROUGH MUTUAL RELATIONSHIP

Our search for Christ-Sophia leads us to a theology of ministry based on our mutual need for new life. Everyone involved in ministry both gives and receives. The reciprocal process circles round and round so that giving and receiving become indistinguishable. One of the critical tasks facing feminist spirituality and ministry is to find compelling images of shared power.[7]

The image of Christ-Sophia holds promise for inspiring a ministry committed to social justice through shared power. The name "Christ-Sophia" suggests equal connection instead of dominance and submission in a relationship. The name "Christ-Sophia" also suggests a connecting bridge between Judaism and Christianity in that it links the figure of Wisdom from Jewish wisdom literature with Jesus of the New Testament. Christ-Sophia images the equal connection between male and female in that the name "Christ" has traditionally denoted male divinity, and "Sophia" is a feminine name for the divine. In addition, Christ-Sophia links races, connecting the Jewish Jesus to Wisdom in both ancient and hellenized Judaism and drawing from both the Egyptian and the Greek figures of Isis.[8]

The image of Christ-Sophia holds promise for empowering a ministry of social justice committed to new life for all people. Through its newness Christ-Sophia underscores the resurrection hope of new life. By incorporating this new name into our worship and ministry, we give testimony to the transforming power of the resurrection. As we experience changes in ourselves and others, we find increased hope that anyone and any condition and any institution has the potential to change.

Jesus taught us to pray, "Your will be done, on earth as it is in heaven" (Mt 6:10). Implied is that perfect justice and peace can be a vision toward which we pray and work. But instead of following Jesus in acting to make the heavenly will a reality on earth, we have projected the injustices of male-dominated culture onto heaven itself. Through our divine symbols, we have deified masculinity and sanctioned a hierarchical, oppressive church and society. By falsely imagining divine will to be a heaven ruled by an exclusively masculine godhead and then praying that earth be like heaven, we have given powerful reinforcement to male supremacy. For God's will of justice to be done on earth, we need new divine images. Christ-Sophia will help bring truth to our vision of heaven and justice to our relationships on earth.

The image of Christ-Sophia holds the power to break down patriarchal structures that keep so many of our sisters and brothers in poverty and oppression. The majority of the poor and starving in the time of Jesus, as well as in the world today, are women. Economic exploitation and patriarchal oppression are two sides of the same coin.[9] Masculine images of the deity have played a crucial part in the sanctioning of male-dominated social, economic, and religious structures. Cultures which have imaged the deity as exclusively masculine have relegated women to subordinate roles in the social order. Jeanne Achterberg demonstrates that only in those cultures that picture the reigning deity as feminine, bisexual, or androgynous have women been able to exercise the healing arts with freedom and power.[10] By connecting the feminine and masculine in mutual relationship, Christ-Sophia offers new possibilities for shared ministry dedicated to healing oppressed individuals and changing oppressive systems.

Speaking the name "Christ-Sophia" in our worship rituals and everyday experience empowers our ministry of resurrection. Language carries profound importance in biblical theology. Just as God spoke the universe into existence, our words hold creative, transforming power. We complete the creative process as we follow our words into redemptive action. Christ-Sophia challenges us to carry our words into acts of ministry and reconciliation. Christ-Sophia models mutual ministry based on the sacredness of all life and on the hope of resurrection for all creation.

SEEKING JUSTICE
THROUGH MUTUAL MINISTRIES

Christ-Sophia empowers ministries of social justice such as Habitat for Humanity. Habitat finds impetus in mutual relationships and multiple connections. This ministry connects poor and rich, female and male, Jew and Christian, Democratic and Republican, unskilled and skilled, uneducated and educated. This diverse group of people come together with the common purpose of providing decent housing. Founders Linda and Millard Fuller have a vision of eliminating inadequate housing all over the world. Habitat respects the dignity of all people and builds self-esteem by helping people help themselves. People help build their own homes which they buy at cost with a no-interest loan. Then they give sweat equity in the form of five hundred hours of labor on the homes of others. One woman tells of discoveries she made through the ministry of Habitat for Humanity: "As I worked with people to rebuild their neighborhood, house by house, partnership by partnership, I discovered connections. I found that I have much in common with the people in this neighborhood. They care as much about the quality of their children's education as I care about the education of mine. We share a vision of good things for our children."

As I was beginning to glimpse Christ-Sophia's vision of social justice, I had the opportunity of ministering to children in an inner city neighborhood. This neighborhood was rich in racial and socio-economic diversity, but it was poor in financial and social resources. I quickly discovered that ministry in this neighborhood would be meaningless and patronizing unless I tried to establish mutual relationships with community leaders and parents. In an effort to model mutuality in our leadership style, the other pastor and I included leaders from the neighborhood. Together with parents who expressed interest, we developed enrichment programs for children. One of these was a summer enrichment program we called "Talents Alive," designed to nurture the artistic gifts of children deprived of cultural opportunities. We offered piano, drama, art, storytelling, films, and field trips. As the children's creative talents blossomed, their self-worth and sense of responsibility also increased.

Another enrichment program, called "Adopt-A-Friend," brought children and adults together. The adults provided transportation to and from church. They also gave the youngsters small gifts, sent them birthday cards, and stayed in touch through telephone calls. The children gave hugs and enthusiasm to their elderly friends, along with calls and prayers when they were sick. We chose the term "Adopt-A-Friend," instead of "Adopt-A-Child," to emphasize the mutuality of the relationship. Both children and adults adopted a friend. They all gave and received the nurturing and companionship of friendship. After just three weeks of being in church with his special friend, a nine-year-old boy said, "This is my favorite place in all the world to come!" After being friends with twin girls for six months, one woman said, "They give me so much love. I never realized how attached I would become to them." These enrichment programs for children thus became enrichment programs for adults as well. All experienced enrichment through the bringing together of a diversity of personalities, cultures, races, ages, and gifts.

One of the key principles of this Christ-Sophia ministry of social justice involves respecting the individual's freedom of choice. Ministry flowing from the example of Jesus, the incarnation of Christ-Sophia, does not force itself on people. Jesus never violated the individual freedom and integrity of persons. Before reaching out with healing to a man who had been ill for thirty-eight years, Jesus asked him, "Do you want to be made well?" (Jn 5:6). The man replied that he had no one to put him into the pool of Bethzatha which was believed to bring healing when the water was stirred. Jesus challenged him to act for his own healing: "Stand up, take your mat and walk" (Jn 5:8). As he did so, he discovered healing.

As a hospital chaplain, I minister as part of a healing team to people who have various illnesses. One of the most challenging of these patients was a woman who had been ill for almost twenty years. Physicians had given her a variety of diagnoses from eating disorder to multiple environmental sensitivity to gastrointestinal disorder. Malnutrition over a long period of time had also resulted in pulmonary problems. When I first saw her, she was preparing for pulmonary surgery. She impressed me as a bright, articulate woman who seemed conflicted over her need to control and her need to be dependent on others. She told me, as well as her family and friends, exactly what she wanted us to do for her. As I left, she told me with a note of pleading in her voice that she wanted me to come to see her the next day.

During the long months of her hospital stay, this woman became a major challenge for the entire healing team. She became demanding and manipulative with nurses, physicians, social workers, and chaplains. We held many case conferences and called in consultants from many medical specialties, including psychiatry. There was some disagreement among the team members as to whether her illness was primarily physiological or psychological. I saw it as equally involving her body, mind, and spirit. From my perspective, it did not so much matter whether her illness originated from an eating disorder or from sensitivity to environmental pollution. Regardless of its origin, this illness had affected her mind and spirit as much as her body. She had become dependent upon her illness as well as upon health care givers, while at the same time resenting and resisting her dependency.

Along with social workers and other team members, I tried to help her focus on wellness instead of illness. We asked such questions as, "What did you do before you were sick? What would it feel like for you to be well again? What are your gifts and goals and dreams? What do you want to do when you are well?" We found that she would answer these questions in a cursory, perfunctory way, and then offer a detailed description of the history of her clinical condition, followed by a thorough analysis of her current symptoms and treatment. We finally came to see that her illness had become her whole life. Tragically, she had come to the point of needing her illness, of depending upon her illness for her identity.

Remembering Jesus' question to the man who had been ill for thirty-eight years, I one day asked this woman, "Do you want to be well?" She gave a half-hearted affirmative answer, but then continued her long recitation of physical problems. I began to realize that I and other members of the healing team had based our relationship with her on our own assumptions and our own needs for her to get well. We had not respected her freedom of choice. No matter how much we desired her healing and believed that we could work with her toward that healing, she would not get well until she really wanted to be well. Our ministry could not be something we imposed upon her, but must be a participation with her in a healing that she had freely chosen.

Ministry flowing from the image and example of Christ-Sophia involves mutually respectful relationships with those alienated from mainstream society because of their illness, poverty, or behaviors labeled as "anti-social." Elisabeth Schüssler Fiorenza adds "the marginal" to the social category of "the poor" in describing the inclusive nature of Jesus' ministry. Jesus was open to all, especially the outcasts of society and religion, such as tax collectors, prostitutes, and sinners.[11]

When we develop relationships with these so-called outcasts, we often discover that they have been abused and sinned against. One woman with whom I counseled had drifted into the behavior of one-night stands with countless men. She wanted to change this behavior not only because she believed it was socially undesirable, but because she knew it was dangerous to her health. As I heard her story, I learned that she had been abandoned by her father and battered by several husbands. Her promiscuous behavior was a defense against risking more hurt through intimate, long-term relationships. Only as she named the abuse and released its control on her life could she find healing.

Christ-Sophia also invites us to include non-human creation in our healing ministry. This invitation is to count the abused earth as among the "least of these,"— battered, polluted, impoverished, abandoned, and exploited. Our careless and cruel treatment of the earth has marred the beauty of Christ-Sophia's creation. Feeling our interconnectedness with all living beings will move us to work toward our mutual restoration. Non-human and human beings stand together in need of resurrection: "We know that the whole creation has been groaning in labor pains until now; and not only the creation, but we ourselves, who have the first fruits of the Spirit, groan inwardly while we wait for adoption, the redemption of our bodies" (Rom 8:22–23). Matthew Fox suggests a new theological paradigm of Jesus Christ as Mother Earth crucified and resurrected. This "new symbol of Jesus as Mother Earth crucified yet rising holds power to awaken humans to the survival of Mother Earth, to the elimination of matricide, and to their own best selves as mystics, prophets, and creative persons."[12]

The image of Christ-Sophia challenges us to a ministry of social justice in solidarity with all the oppressed. According to Jacquelyn Grant, African-American women best represent "the least," to whom Jesus referred, in that they are the "oppressed of the oppressed."[13] They suffer the triple discrimination of racism, sexism, and classism. Out of their struggle against oppression, however, they are producing some of the most powerful and beautiful works in American literature.[14] In African-American women writers, we are beginning to see that reversal of which Jesus spoke: "But many who are first will be last, and the last will be first" (Mk 10:31).

In spite of all the injustice they have suffered, African-American women have often demonstrated the greatest in human character and creativity. Standing in solidarity with the oppressed begins with hearing their stories. In the sermon, "Come and Walk in My Shoes," Tommye Mitchell, a member of an inclusive worship community in central Texas, invites us to hear her story of the injustices she experienced as an African-American woman. She challenges us to strive together toward new life and justice for all.

COME AND WALK IN MY SHOES
by Tommye Mitchell

An old Indian once said, "I will never undertake to judge people until I have spent ten moons in their moccasins." With this in mind, I have selected as my topic, "Come and Walk in My Shoes."

I'm black. I was born that way. I had nothing to do with the matter. I grew up in the South where segregation was the law of the land, and we black people were reminded that if we wanted to get along, to even survive, we had better remember to stay in our place. And where was our place? It was the back of the bus, the front of the train, the top of the hotel, the bottom of the ship — always somewhere disadvantaged of our white brothers and sisters. If you were black and you were standing you were loitering, if you were sitting you were watching, if you were walking you were loafing, if you were running you were escaping — subject to getting shot in the back. I grew up in a section of town called "Dark Town," a few blocks past where the street lights stopped, the pavement stopped, the running water stopped. Everything seemed to stop where the white folks stopped. Come, if you will, and walk in my shoes.

Everywhere we look we are faced with abhorrence of everything that is black. Bad news comes bordered in black. Storm clouds are black. Mourning clothes are black. If people don't want you in their organization, they black ball you. If you offend someone, you make their black list. Black cake is devil's food, but white cake is angel food. If a black cat crosses your trail, there are people who say that it's bad luck.

Down through the years black has had a negative connotation. In spite of all this, black people have made great contributions in every period of our history. Charles Drew discovered a way to preserve blood plasma in blood banks. Garrett Morgan invented the automatic stoplight, and Ernst Matzeliger invented the first shoe-lasting machine. Architect Paul Williams designed the Los Angeles airport and countless homes for movie stars. Dr. Dan Williams was the first to stitch the human heart. We have too many outstanding athletes and musicians, too many mayors and other important government officials to name. In spite of all of this, people are inclined to see African-Americans as inferior, unable, and incapable.

The story is told about a certain plumber who went out to a very affluent neighborhood to do a little plumbing job. It was one of those fancy neighborhoods that had the tall brick fence and security gate. You couldn't even go in unless you went past the guard house. All the houses out there were $500,000 plus. The plumber went into the neighborhood and passed the most beautiful lawn he'd ever seen. The lawn was so pretty he felt compelled to go back. There was a black man working in the yard, and the plumber stopped his little red pick-up and said, "What you say there, boy? You sure know what to do with a yard. I wish I had a boy like you. How much do you get for keeping a yard like this?" He said, "I get to sleep and eat with the lady inside. She's my wife." You see, never in his wildest imagination did the plumber conceive that this beautiful home and manicured lawn could have been owned by a black.

To be black is to have one strike against you. To be black and female is to have two strikes. Come and walk with me in my shoes. It is amazing how the lives of blacks and women have paralleled one another. Like blacks, women have been reminded that we should stay in our place. To be a woman is to have people make derogatory remarks even in your presence. You hear them say, "You drive like a woman"; "You think like a woman." Even in the 1990s, sometimes it seems that our expectations for women are low, and often we program our girls to have low aspirations. We say to them, "You are a woman. Be charming, be gentle, be sweet. Have a big heart, but a little brain. You can do things, but not too well. You can aspire, but not too high." And we say to our boys, "You are a man. Be strong, be powerful. Be mind, not heart, for heart is for woman. Be arrogant, be aggressive, never cry. Be a man."

Many of us think that it is all right for a woman to be a school supervisor, but not a school superintendent. How many female school superintendents do you know? We think it is all right for her to be a surgical nurse, but not the surgeon. It is all right for her to be the teacher, but not the preacher. It is all right for her to be the flight attendant, but not the pilot. It is all right for her to do small things, but not the large things. There are still many people who would not vote for a woman for president of this country, no matter what her qualifications. And invariably, when we look for the boss, we are not looking for a woman — or a black.

Salespersons come to my son's business. They see my son behind the counter and they say, "I'd like to see the manager, please," because a black is not supposed to be the manager. When he says, "I am the manager," they ask, "Well, is the owner in?" Surely a black man under the age of twenty-five cannot be the owner of a business. Maybe by some chance, he could be the manager.

Sexism and racism are as American as apple pie. Come and walk in my shoes. One day we shall overcome.

Jesus wanted women to be all that we could be. He made his position very clear when Mary was sitting at his feet philosophizing and asking questions. Martha wanted Jesus to order Mary into the kitchen to help with the work, but Jesus said, "Martha, Martha, you are worried and distracted by many things; there is need of only one thing. Mary has chosen the better part, which will not be taken away from her" (Lk 10:41–42). Mary was using her mind and thinking about things eternal, because no matter how much you cook and eat today, you're going to be hungry tomorrow. No matter how much you scrub and clean, it can't last. Soon it will be dirty again.

Jesus must have known the problems women would face in the days ahead, for on his way to die on the cross, he stopped and said to the women by the side of the road, "Daughters of Jerusalem, do not weep for me, but weep for yourselves and for your children" (Lk 23:28).

Oh, come and walk in my shoes. I thank God for my experience as a black woman, for all people are my friends. Those who love me teach me tenderness. Those who hate me teach me caution. Those who are indifferent to me teach me self-reliance.

Every book I used in public school was a second-hand book — dirty, torn-up, and out-of-date. I learned to do the best I could with what I had, wherever I was. Even in the days of lynching, I learned to love, if not because of, in spite of. I was taught never to let anyone drag me so low as to make me hate, for hate is like burning down your own house to kill a rat.

We were taught about our heritage, and photos of black heroines and heroes lined our walls. We learned about women like Sojourner Truth, who was not free until she was thirty and who spoke out for what she believed. She spoke out for women's rights, for temperance, and for the abolition of slavery. She was invited to address the Women's Suffrage Convention which convened in Akron, Ohio, in 1851. She said to the white women, "We came over on different ships, but we're practically in the same boat." In the middle of the nineteenth century a white woman had no rights that a white man was duty-bound to respect. Like blacks, women were denied the right to vote and denied the right to educational opportunities. If a woman worked, her husband could pick up her check and spend it as he saw fit. If her father died and willed her some property, her husband could dispose of it as he saw fit. A man could send his children abroad to study without his wife's consent. Even in the case of a divorce, the man got custody of the children.

Harriet Tubman got sick and tired of slavery. She knew it was not right and she thought: "Before I would remain a slave, I'd rather be dead and in my grave and go home to God and be free." She devised a plan to escape and told her husband about it. He said, "You can't do that. Ain't no woman got no business runnin' off into the night. We got a roof over our head and all the chicken feet and heads we can eat and plenty of syrup to sop and plenty of rags to sleep on and Ol' Master never beats us over twice a week, and you talk about runnin' away. We doin' all right. The next time you talk foolish like this I'm gonna report you to da Master." But you know, she traveled from Maryland to Pennsylvania, walking by night and hiding by day. When she reached her destination, she told of her plan to go back and help others to escape. Surely some people told her, "You can't go back. You better let well enough do." With a price of forty thousand dollars on her head, wanted dead or alive, she returned to the South over thirty times and helped over three hundred slaves escape to freedom!

What can we learn from this great woman? She had a dream. But she had more than a dream. She had a plan. It's all right to build castles in the sky, but you need to put foundations under them. She knew no discouragement. She presented no alibi. She believed in God, and with her Bible in her hand, she said, "Even though I walk through the darkest valley, I fear no evil; for you are with me" (Ps 23:4). Harriet Tubman knew how to rally people to the cause. Not just black people, but white people furnished transportation by designing false-bottom boats, and by furnishing food, shelter, training, and jobs. She could not have done this by herself. She knew how to rally people to the cause.

Sometimes a woman or a black gets on the board, the council, or the commission, and she or he gets an "I'm-on-the-board" attitude, not realizing that they have just one vote, unless they develop the expertise to rally people to the cause. The men on the board simply get together at the hunting lodge and fuss and cuss and discuss, until the wee hours of the morning, until they're all in one accord. And when they come to the meeting, the chairperson says, "Is there any discussion?" Have you ever wondered why there's no discussion? They've already discussed the matter! This meeting is just a formality, so that what goes on can go into the minutes. Wake up, and get wise!

We must go forth and teach our children not only the game, but the games people play. We must teach them to love, for God is love. We must teach them to study, for far too many want knowledge without study. We must teach them to work, for far too many want wealth without work. We must teach them that excellence is a commodity that's always in demand, and only the ignorant will question its color or its sex. We must teach them that to wear the crown, they have to bear the cross. For one day Jesus will come and say, "Not woman, not man, not black, not white, not Korean, not Mexican, but servant, servant, you who have been faithful over a few things, come on up. I'll make you ruler over many things."

QUESTIONS FOR
REFLECTION AND DISCUSSION

1. What do you see as the major social justice issues of our day?

2. In what ways could a theology founded on the resurrected Christ-Sophia empower a ministry of social justice?

3. How does the image of Christ-Sophia suggest mutual relationship?

4. Can you think of other divine images that could inspire shared power in the ministry of social justice?

5. How do exclusively masculine images of God sanction injustice in church and society?

6. What experiences of ministry have been most satisfying to you?

7. In what ways could a theology of ministry flowing from the image of Christ-Sophia change your ministry?

CHAPTER 7

The Church of Christ-Sophia

"So we, who are many, are one body in Christ [-Sophia], and individually we are members one of another." (Romans 12:5)

The resurrected Christ-Sophia dwells not only in individuals, but also in communities. The search for new life moves to the corporate expression of our faith in Christian communities which embody the risen One. The Spirit of Christ-Sophia extends beyond the individual, finding full expression in community. The metaphor of the faith community as the Body of Christ-Sophia becomes prominent in New Testament christology: "Now you are the body of Christ [-Sophia] and individually members of it" (1 Cor 12:27).

The fact that the risen One is embodied in and finds saving expression through a community made up of both women and men means that the Savior of human beings is not just the one historical male, Jesus of Nazareth. "Christians, women and men, need not turn to a male savior with all the patriarchal implications this would have."[1] The image of Christ-Sophia offers females and males more than a male savior. Basic to the spirituality of men, as well as women, is this movement beyond a male savior who sanctions male-dominated systems. The Christian community, composed of female and male members in equal relationship, embodies the saving Christ-Sophia alive today. The church plays a major role in the ongoing process of salvation.

Edward Schillebeeckx articulates the Catholic doctrine of the church as the sacrament of the risen Christ when he points out that the earthly church is the visible realization of Christ's saving work in history. In Catholic theology, the church is not merely a means of salvation, but it is salvation itself. Schillebeeckx emphasizes that it is not only the ecclesiastical hierarchy but the whole community of the faithful that form the sacramental realization of Christ on earth. The church in its entirety serves as the redeeming presence of Christ.[2] It is thus a strange contradiction that Catholic doctrine dictates that the priestly hierarchy must be male, but that the Christian community can be female and male. Th Vatican's Sacred Congregation for the Doctrine of the Faith declared that there must be a "natural resemblance" between Christ and the person who offers the sacraments, and that if a woman performed this priestly role, "it would be difficult to see in the minister the image of Christ. For Christ himself was and remains a man."[3] If the church in its entirety is "the sacramental or mystical Christ,"[4] as Schillebeeckx states, would it not follow that the members of the church must also be male, because "Christ himself was and remains a man"?

The risen Christ-Sophia includes male and female qualities. Christ-Sophia includes all baptized members of the church. In baptism women, like men, put on Christ. But they do not become male. The living Christ therefore cannot be solely male. If Christ were solely male, then women could not be baptized, nor could Europeans, African-Americans, Native Americans, Euro-Americans, or anyone else who did not duplicate the physical characteristics of the historical Jesus. In fact, only Jewish males could be baptized as Christians. Through baptism women share the identity of Christ in exactly the same way and to the same extent that men do.[5] Thus we see again the importance of the name "Christ-Sophia" to convey this truth.

A RADICAL EQUALITY

Egalitarianism is an essential principle of an ecclesiology flowing from the centrality of Christ-Sophia. To be truly the Body of Christ-Sophia, a church needs to practice equality of all persons. The church's leadership and ministry should be based on people's gifts and talents, not on the status presumptions of a patriarchal structure. The church seeking to embody the risen Christ-Sophia thus must break down the hierarchic organizational structures in which some members are higher and some are lower. The distinction between clergy and laity disappears as women seek ordination for the ultimate goal of dissolving the division between ordained and nonordained members. As one clergywoman said to a group of women considering ordination, "We have to have power in order to give it away." The ordination of women is not for the incorporation of some women into positions of authority in the existing hierarchy, but "for the conversion of the whole church to the discipleship community of equals that Jesus initiated."[6]

The apostolic churches functioned as communities of equals. The church birthed by the Spirit of Christ-Sophia on the day of Pentecost followed a revolutionary vision of equality. Peter proclaimed that Joel's prophecy was being fulfilled: The Spirit was pouring out power "upon all flesh" (Acts 2:17). Daughters and sons, old and young, all classes of people received the ordaining of the Spirit (Acts 2:17–18). At Pentecost the Spirit empowered believers to live out the discipleship of equals initiated by Jesus. The church of the first century thrived on shared power.

The Body of Christ-Sophia today rejects dominating power and affirms shared power. Members of the Christian community seeking to embody the message of Christ-Sophia can develop their own sense of authority about their faith experiences and their own power in shaping the community of faith.[7] The Body becomes fragmented and impoverished if only a few people hold power and exercise gifts. It is not enough for laypeople simply to "help out" the clergy with the ministry of the church. All members are called to be ministers, to be priests to one another and to the world.[8] Bringing together diverse people in equal partnership within the community of faith restores wholeness to the Body of Christ-Sophia.

THE FREE EXERCISE OF DIVERSE GIFTS

Christ-Sophia inspires an ecclesiology that brings wholeness through the free exercise of diverse gifts within the community. As the embodiment of the risen Christ-Sophia, the church affirms a unity of humanity. Such unity is not an oppressive or leveling unity, but one which allows individual differences to develop according to gifts, not stereotypes. Unity grows from a community of persons who are diverse and yet have freely joined together as sisters and brothers. The Pauline metaphor of the Body indicates the creative tension between the ordered life of the church and the diversity of the expression of members' gifts. Essential to the functioning of the Body of Christ-Sophia is the diversity of gifts, equally valued for their contribution to the whole. Members then have equal opportunity to exercise their gifts and gain equal respect (Rom 12:4–8; Eph 4:4–16). All gifts have equal importance in the Body of Christ-Sophia; there is no hierarchy of ministries (1 Cor 12:4–27).

The church of Christ-Sophia celebrates the creative gifts of all members and encourages the discovery of new gifts through interdependent activity. Shared ritual-making, for example, nourishes creativity and accentuates the value of all individuals.[9] Coming together with others to create rituals opens our imaginations to new forms of worship that engage our senses as well as our minds. When all members freely contribute their gifts, worship services can abound with dance, poetry, music, drama, and other art forms. In this way worship can awaken our whole body-mind-spirits. Matthew Fox laments that most white worship in Western society excludes the body. He says that until we bring the body back into our worship, the Body of Christ is "only an idea in the head. The Cosmic Christ wants to dance, to express itself bodily, to respond to Good News and to cosmic grace."[10]

The church of Christ-Sophia depends upon all members contributing the gifts of our whole selves, body-mind-spirit. The name "Christ-Sophia" vividly symbolizes embodied spiritual experience. "Christ" suggests both incarnated and resurrected deity. "Sophia" implies the integration of mind and feelings in deity. Sophia is the voice of Wisdom expressed with great passion. Sophia expresses feelings of impatience and anger over the human failure to listen to her reason (Prv 1:20-25). The image of Christ-Sophia also evokes rituals related to human experience. These rituals may involve symbols drawn from daily life, such as quilts, or celebrate passages of life, such as puberty and child-bearing.[11] New possibilities unfold as new symbols become part of the community's life and worship. The very invoking of the name "Christ-Sophia" startles us out of our worn-out forms and formulas, and invites us to experience resurrection in our community life.

TRANSFORMATION OF INDIVIDUALS AND COMMUNITIES

An ecclesiology flowing from the centrality of Christ-Sophia leads to transformation. This transformation begins as the experience of each individual takes on new meaning and value in the context of the faith community. Within the community each member's experience becomes sacred reality as it is heard and affirmed by other members. As we feel that others value our experience, we begin to discover that our lives are sacred. We begin to appreciate all our experiences more deeply and to reflect upon divine action in our lives.[12] Because human life is communal, we need a community to affirm the redemptive life we experience.[13] Connecting with others on our spiritual journey increases our faith and hope. Insights from others in the community often transform our thinking and our behavior. The community validates our insights and experiences, and pushes us beyond the limits of tradition. Sharing our reflections on Christ-Sophia with one another deepens our wisdom.

Focusing on the image of Christ-Sophia transforms Christian communities as well as the individuals within them. Christ-Sophia leads communities to change from hierarchic to egalitarian structures, from exclusive to inclusive leadership, and from rigid, intellectual liturgies to creative, holistic worship. Often these transformations occur first in small alternative communities and only later in more structured church bodies. Women-Church provides one example of such a community as it establishes bases for a feminist culture and celebrational community. Although Women-Church has autonomy from traditional churches, it does not advocate total separation from the institutional church. Rather the creative dialectic between these alternative communities and traditional institutions holds promise for transforming and redefining the meaning of church.[14]

Christian basic ecclesial communities, begun in Latin America, provide another example of alternative community. Although basic ecclesial communities have sought to transform oppressive systems through liberation theology, they have largely ignored the plight of women. Anne Andersson believes these communities could also become liberating for women through the addition of feminist hermeneutics and feminist symbolism, such as that linking Sophia with Christ.[15] Whether through these alternative communities or within traditional communities, Christ-Sophia holds power for transforming the Christian community.

Christ-Sophia's resurrection power extends beyond the individual and the Christian community to encompass the world community. Christ-Sophia inspires us to dream of a world free of poverty, hunger, exploitation, domination, oppression, and violence. The faith community can serve as a mediator of our dreams. The community helps us link our hopes to Christ-Sophia's dream of a world healed of poverty, injustice, and domination.[16] Our hopes and dreams gain power as we join in community with other dreamers. Through the faith community our dreams develop focus so that we can move them into reality. Instead of becoming overwhelmed by the magnitude of the needs in our world, we join with others in taking specific actions that lead to concrete change.

AN INCLUSIVE
WORSHIP COMMUNITY EXPERIENCE

A community that is focused and founded on the image of Christ-Sophia welcomes change that leads to new life for all. Such a community invites the members to a continual seeking of Christ-Sophia alive in the world today. This search can take place in many different settings although specific, local communities may best be able to embody the ideals that are central to the image of Christ-Sophia.

In central Texas, I experienced an intentional Christian community committed to an ecclesiology of egalitarianism, free exercise of gifts, and transformation. For four years this community gathered weekly to provide an alternative to patriarchal, hierarchic, segregated churches. Weary of the stifling atmosphere present in many traditional churches, we began a community open to the fresh movement of the Spirit. At the beginning we called ourselves an

"Alternative Worship Community: intentionally integrated, deliberately inclusive in language, and open to all people." When our commitment to gender and racial inclusiveness became clear, we dropped this cumbersome title to become simply the "Inclusive Worship Community."

Believing that hierarchies stifled the movement of the Spirit, the Inclusive Worship Community had no single leader. Instead, every member of the community exercised leadership according to her or his gifts. There was no paid staff; all served as volunteers. Members rotated leadership responsibilities. The unique gifts of members provided a variety of worship forms and styles. Some services followed a formal order with sermon, litanies, hymns, and scripture readings. Such services resembled traditional services except that language and leadership were inclusive in race and gender. Other services featured liturgical dance, drama, art, guided meditation, dialogue sermons, and book studies. Members encouraged one another to create new songs, poetry, meditations, and other worship aids.

The setting for the Inclusive Worship Community likewise varied according to the movement of the Spirit expressed through the diversity of the community. Because many of the members were active in other church communities, our choice of meeting times had limitations. We agreed to meet early Sunday morning before activities began at other churches. Our place of meeting moved from the sanctuary of a predominantly white church to an outdoor park to the sanctuary of a predominantly black church. In warm weather the park provided the perfect setting for informal participation, meditation, and movement inspired by the beauty of creation. Worship set in the predominantly black church sanctuary gave a clearer message of our commitment to racial inclusiveness.

A big challenge throughout the life of our Inclusive Worship Community was making our ideal of egalitarianism a reality. Since we had no paid leaders, our community depended upon members' voluntarily assuming responsibility according to their diverse gifts. In an ideal situation, leadership would be equally shared. In reality, some accepted leadership more readily than others. Often the unspoken expectation was that those of us with theological education would take more responsibility for the worship services. At times all of us wanted to fall back on our conditioning as church spectators and leave the leadership to others.

One of our greatest challenges was the bringing together of people with diverse concerns to work toward the ideal of inclusiveness. An African-American sociologist serving on the committee initiating the inclusive community expressed concern that the majority of black females and males did not see inclusive language as an issue. Although she saw the importance of inclusive language to gender and racial justice, she had trouble getting other African-Americans even to discuss the issue. Most dismissed it as a concern of white middle-class women.

Susan Brooks Thistlethwaite sheds light on the differences between black and white women on the issue of inclusive language. She observes that many black female seminarians object to white feminist guidelines on inclusive language, especially those concerning references to God as "Father" and "Lord." Father-language for God has not concerned black women writers to the degree that it has white feminists because black churches put equal emphasis on the Spirit and the Lord. Black Christians use "Lord" to refer to Jesus, whom they see as both "mother to the motherless, and father to the fatherless." Although black churches are not generally egalitarian in language or leadership, they have developed a religious symbolism that is more gender-inclusive than that common in white churches. Thistlethwaite calls not only for respect of differences in the experiences of black and white women, but for the use of these differences as the starting point for white feminist theology.[17]

The Inclusive Worship Community strove to respect and celebrate differences, while seeking connections. We found it easier, however, to welcome differences in style than in language. One of the reasons some of us became involved in the Inclusive Worship Community was so that we would have a place where we felt ourselves affirmed and included in worship. If we heard masculine language for God, we questioned the value of the community for our spirituality.

The Inclusive Worship Community, nevertheless, struggled to combine the ideals of racial and gender inclusiveness in its search for the risen Christ-Sophia. Listening to one another brought deeper respect for differences, while also building bridges. In her book,

White Women's Christ and Black Women's Jesus, Jacquelyn Grant guided us in our understanding of differences. White feminist theology, based on white women's experience, fails to understand the role Jesus has played in the lives of black women and men. Womanist theology, based on black women's experience, reveals the degree of identification of black women with Jesus' undeserved suffering. In the parable of the Last Judgment in Matthew chapter 25, Jesus identifies with "the least of these." The "least" locates the condition of black women, who suffer the triple discrimination of racism, sexism, and classism. Grant and other womanist theologians locate Christ in the black women's community: "Christ, found in the experiences of black women, is a black woman."[18] Grant's theology helped white feminists within the Inclusive Worship Community understand that when black women preach and sing about Jesus, using all masculine pronouns, they also experience Jesus as female and black. This understanding served as a starting point for introducing feminine divine language.

In one service in which the community focused on the image of Mother God, one woman from a conservative, predominantly black church background testified to the power of this image for her spirituality. When she was a young girl, this African-American woman had lost her mother. Her father had reared her and her siblings. The picture of a Mother God deeply moved her by filling the void in her childhood. She wept as she said, "For the first time I touched the feminine face of God. Now I feel that I have a Mother and a model for being a mother myself." She went on to tell of the profound love and acceptance she felt when she touched the face of Mother God. The whole community in turn felt affirmed and empowered by the eloquent testimony of this woman.

The Inclusive Worship Community also helped men to grow in their appreciation of feminine images of God. A black male minister identified with the issues I raised in the book, *In Whose Image? God and Gender.* Growing up with pictures of Jesus and God as white, he had experienced feelings of distance and alienation from God. Black liberation theology had helped him to image God as black, and consequently to feel more profoundly than ever the biblical message that he is formed in the image of God and that God is for him. He told me that as he was reading my book, he felt a deep connection with women. If women see pictures only of a male God and Christ and hear only masculine God-language, then they must have feelings similar to those a white God evoked in him. This African-American minister, who had felt empowered by imaging God as black, thus began to feel with women the power of imaging God as female.

This minister became evangelistic in spreading his new insight among his colleagues. He met much resistance to gender-inclusive ministry and language. Undaunted, he gave copies of my book to many of his colleagues and invited me to give a book review to the Interdenominational Ministerial Alliance meeting. Attending this meeting were fifteen African-American men and one African-American woman. One of the men was especially open and receptive to my ideas. After the meeting, we talked about many points raised at the meeting. Since he was so enthusiastic about inclusive language and ministry, I told him about the Inclusive Worship Community. Several months later he invited the community to meet in the facilities of the church he pastored.

His involvement in the community, along with the use of this new meeting place, contributed to our search for the risen Christ-Sophia through the inclusive faith community. It also helped in our effort to become a more racially balanced community. In the process of experiencing a diversity of gifts and worship styles, we felt the fresh wind of the Spirit. We discovered that we shared the pain of traditions and institutions that have stifled the Spirit of Christ-Sophia within us.

On the surface it may seem quite natural for oppressed groups in a patriarchal society to come together to work toward the common causes of freedom and equal opportunity. But as we try to make connections, we continue to discover obstacles. Rosemary Radford Ruether analyzes the psychology of such resistance: "The whole psychology of oppression and the social structure of oppression is to set the oppressed in multiple relationships of intrastructural tension and therefore to allow most of the control to take place by the way the oppressed control each other."[19] Thus, instead of working together, we find one AHANA group (African, Hispanic, Asian, Native American) opposing another, and AHANA men opposing equality for women.[20]

While recognizing the need for separatist groups to analyze specific kinds of oppression and to empower specific groups, the Inclusive Worship Community found its purpose in bringing people together. Malcolm X served an important role by teaching separation of African-Americans to foster black self-love and self-determination. He believed that African-Americans could gain power by uniting with one another, not with other races. "He contended that there could be no unity among the different races based on equality until there was first a unity of particular races among their own kind."[21] Ruether advocates a similar separation and uniting of women into faith and worship communities called "Women-Church." These communities foster women's self-esteem and self-determination by honestly critiquing patriarchy and developing new symbols and liturgies for the nurture and empowerment of women.[22] Elsewhere Ruether states that each oppressed group needs to analyze its own specific problems and then to relate them to those of other groups. Only when these problems are "drawn out in their particularities and we relate them to each other do we begin to get a total picture of what oppression is all about."[23] The Inclusive Worship Community sought to bring groups together to relate specific experiences of oppression in order to find understanding and the power to bring change.

Sojourner Truth served as a model of someone who united people in order to overcome racial and gender oppression. Though best known for her contributions to the anti-slavery movement, she turned the tide for women at the Woman's Rights Convention in Ohio in 1851. Some of the women tried to keep her from speaking because they were afraid that their cause would be "mixed with abolition and niggers," and they would thus "be utterly denounced."[24] But when the men came close to taking over the meeting and silencing the women, Sojourner Truth rose to speak. She demolished their arguments concerning the weakness of women by pointing out the double standard: She and other black women had never been helped into carriages or spared any physical labor. In addition, she refuted their theological arguments about the superiority of man because of the manhood of Christ: "Where did your Christ come from? From God and a woman. Man had nothing to do with him."[25] Frances D. Gage, who was presiding at the meeting, said that Sojourner Truth's message brought "roars of applause" and left "more than one of us with streaming eyes and hearts beating with gratitude. She had taken us up in her strong arms and carried us safely over the slough of difficulty, turning the whole tide in our favor."[26] Because she had experienced the double oppression of being a woman and a person who had been enslaved because of her color, Sojourner Truth was able to combine the causes of racial and gender freedom in her preaching.

Other nineteenth-century American women became models for our Inclusive Worship Community. We saw that the causes of abolition and women's suffrage were closely related. White women who began working for the freedom of the black race soon discovered that they had to defend their own liberty to speak out against the evils of slavery. Sarah and Angelina Grimke were two early leaders who combined the causes of racial and gender freedom. In advocating liberty for the black race, Sarah and Angelina had to defend their own right of free speech against clergymen and others who believed that women should keep silent. Soon other women came to see the inseparability of freedom for black slaves and freedom for themselves. "In the early Anti-Slavery conventions, the broad principles of human rights were so exhaustively discussed, justice, liberty, and equality so clearly taught, that women who crowded to listen, readily learned the lesson of freedom for themselves."[27]

Although Martin Luther King's acceptance of patriarchal values prevented his seeing the connection between racism and sexism, he preached ideals of freedom and justice that led to such connection. Dorothy Cotton, who worked closely with King in the Southern Christian Leadership Conference, believed that King would have come to see women as an oppressed class.[28] Rejecting the separatist philosophy of Malcolm X, King worked toward a fully integrated society where every person would be equal. He preached his dream that one day "little black boys and black girls will be able to join hands with little white boys and white girls as sisters and brothers."[29]

Although we affirmed the continued need for separatist groups that strengthen self-esteem and identity, the Inclusive Worship Community found its purpose in joining hands as sisters and brothers to work toward the ideals of justice and unity. We understood and respected the viewpoints of those who believe that the cause of racial justice is diluted if it is joined with the cause of gender justice, and of those who believe that women constantly diffuse their power by taking care of the needs of other individuals and groups. At times during the life of the community many of us felt the truth of such views. But we also discovered the power of connecting with one another to understand and overcome the forces of oppression.

One such powerful experience of connection came during a service focusing on healing for women who had been victims of violence. An African-American minister shared his feelings of connection with women who had been raped. He spoke of the rape of the entire African-American race, and then went on to identify with the psychological dynamics of raped women. Like these women, he had gone through denial for the sake of survival and then the anger that comes with recognition of the violence. With deep feeling in his voice he read the following description of a white woman who had been raped by an unknown man in a ski mask while she was taking trash to a dump near a woods:

> During the rape she became convinced that she would die and resigned herself to her impending death. But when the rapist left and she found herself still alive, prone on the ground, she experienced all around herself a sudden and compelling vision of Christ as a crucified woman. As she lay transfixed by this vision, an enormous relief swept over her and she realized that she would not have to explain to a male God that she had been raped. God knew what it was like to be a woman who had been raped....Just as women have been able to experience themselves in the crucified rabbi from Nazareth, men must be able to experience Christ in the raped woman.[30]

As he read this account, it became clear that this black male was experiencing Christ-Sophia in the raped woman.

Such deep connections led to new discoveries of Christ-Sophia alive in the world today. In spite of many obstacles, the Inclusive Worship Community held on to its vision of the freeing of all human beings and all creation to become all God created them to be as

they live in peace and mutual relationship. In searching for the resurrected Christ-Sophia, we laid the foundation for changes needed
to make this vision reality. The Inclusive Worship Community
worked for change at the deepest levels of attitude. We discovered
the risen Christ-Sophia when we found new ways of thinking and
feeling. We found Christ-Sophia when we transformed stifling, crip-
pling traditions into life-giving, liberating experiences. We discovered Christ-Sophia when we made new connections that
empowered us to work together toward the vision. New life is the
very essence of the resurrected Christ-Sophia. Wherever we discovered new life, we discovered Christ-Sophia. As we worked together as a community to bring new life, we felt that Christ-Sophia
gave us power.

Although we lost the security of predictable structures and leadership in our Inclusive Worship Community, we gained the freedom to develop our gifts. In the process we discovered creative gifts
we did not know we had. Our openness to the spontaneity of the
Spirit of Christ-Sophia brought us surprise blessings. We learned
the importance of equal participation not just for fairness, but for
the enrichment that comes through experiencing a diversity of gifts.
We felt barriers breaking down as we developed mutual relationships. Our Inclusive Worship Community also had a witness
in other organizations in which members were involved. From experiences of empowerment in our worship community, we went
forth as ministers of justice and peace into the larger community.

Chapter nine of this book offers a treasury of worship resources
for inclusive communities. Of special importance is the service for
"Birthing an Inclusive Worship Community" (pages 136-42) which
embodies the ideas and ideals for Inclusive Worship Communities
expressed in this chapter.

QUESTIONS FOR
REFLECTION AND DISCUSSION

1. How does an all-male clergy contradict biblical and traditional
teaching concerning the Christian church?

2. The New Testament teaches that Christ continues to live in our world through the church. How does the name "Christ-Sophia" convey this truth?

3. Do you believe in the ordination of women? Why, or why not?

4. In what ways would a church founded on Christ-Sophia be different from your church?

5. Have you tried to initiate changes within your church? How did the church respond?

6. Do you believe you can bring change best by working within the traditional church, by being part of an alternative community, or by doing both?

7. How would you envision a community of faith flowing from the centrality of Christ-Sophia?

PART III

Experiencing the Resurrected Christ-Sophia Through Worship

CHAPTER 8

Following
Christ-Sophia
Through the Seasons

The sacred seasons guide our search for the resurrected Christ-Sophia. Most Christian traditions follow some seasonal pattern, whether or not they strictly follow the liturgical calendar. Celebrations of Christmas and Easter not only have become commonplace in Christian churches, but also have taken a prominent place in our society through commercialization. Observances of Advent, Lent, and Pentecost have retained more of their religious meaning and are less subject to commercialization.

For many Christians seasonal celebrations have lost much of their meaning and impact. Rigid liturgies and lifeless repetition have rendered these "celebrations" spiritually empty and meaningless. By focusing entirely on God's action in the past, they fail to move current-day Christians to an experience of new life.

Through our worship symbols and services, Christmas and Easter have especially become set in the concrete of past events. For a growing number of Christians these worship forms have no life-giving power because they symbolize an exclusively male savior. Through our hymns and prayers and sermons, we keep our eyes mainly on sacred events that took place in history instead of opening our eyes to the meaning of these events for us today. Instead of rejoicing in the inclusiveness of the incarnation and the resurrection, we limit our imaginations to the baby boy in the manger and the historical man Jesus rising from the dead.

The sacred seasons themselves lie in need of resurrection. Through new and creative interpretations and symbols, they can come to life again. Christ-Sophia invites us to experience the seasons of the Christian year in new ways. While retaining cyclical, seasonal patterns as a way of connecting with all creation, liturgy flowing from the image of Christ-Sophia offers new life.

The following prayers and reflections for Advent, Easter, and Pentecost are invitations to creative discovery. They provide alternatives to those more standard worship forms that many people find stifling and exclusive. A continual search for the resurrected Christ-Sophia can lead us through the sacred seasons to new life.

ADVENT: BIRTHING CHRIST-SOPHIA

Rich with images of hope and pregnancy and birthing, Advent offers exciting new possibilities. The inclusion of feminine symbols and language flows naturally from these images into Advent celebrations. In the biblical story, Anna and Elizabeth, along with Simeon and Zechariah, symbolize hope and expectancy. Advent takes on new meaning through reflection on Christ-Sophia as the Wisdom who continually gives birth to all things (Wis 7:27).

As individuals and as communities, we all need continual birth into new life. In a Christmas sermon Meister Eckhart said of Christ's birth, "This birth is always happening. And yet, if it does not occur in me, how could it help me? Everything depends on that."[1]

Advent is more than a static event in history. The word "Advent," which means "coming," connotes continual action. Advent offers possibilities of continual sacred activity in our world. Advent opens opportunities for the continual birth of the divine within and among us. Although this birth may be painful and frightening, it brings freedom and joy.[2]

The following Advent liturgy may be used to help people experience the birthing of new life. (See also the Advent drama in the following chapter.)

Call to Rejoicing

All: O come, all ye faithful, joyful and triumphant.

Group 1: O come, let us adore Her.

Group 2: Let us adore Her?

Group 1: O come, let us adore Her.

Group 2: Don't you mean adore Him?

Group 1: The Living Christ we come to praise
          joins both Her and Him
          and more than Them.
          Christ is Gentile and Jew,
          black and white,
          female and male.
          Christ is all and in all.

All: Then come let us adore the Christ
          in you and me,
          the Christ of all,
          who sets us free.
          O come, let us adore Christ.

Biblical Invitation to Wisdom
(from Proverbs 3:13–21; James 1:5)

Reader 1: Happy are those who find Wisdom,
           and those who get understanding.

All: For Her income is better than silver,
           and Her revenue better than gold.

Reader 2: She is more precious than jewels,
           and nothing you desire can compare with Her.

All: Long life is in Her right hand;
            in Her left hand are riches and honor.

Reader 3:   Her ways are ways of pleasantness,
            and all Her paths are peace.

All: She is a tree of life to those who lay hold of Her;
            those who hold Her fast are called happy.

Reader 4:   Wisdom founded the earth and established the heavens.

All: By Wisdom the depths broke open,
            and the clouds drop down dew.

Reader 5:   Sons and daughters, keep sound wisdom and prudence.

All: If any of us is lacking in wisdom, let us ask God, who
            gives to all generously and ungrudgingly, and Wisdom
            will be given us.

Reflection on the Advent of Christ-Sophia

We come on this Sunday in the sacred season of Advent to worship
the One who came into our world to turn things around and set us
right with God and with one another. The word "Advent" means
"coming." It not only means the past coming of Christ almost two
thousand years ago, but the continual coming of Christ into our
world today. Although so many of our Christmas carols and stories
and celebrations focus on Christ's coming in history, let us explore
Christ's coming in the present and discover ways we can participate
in Christ's present coming.

   Christ was and is many things to many people. One of the biblical pictures of Christ that has great potential for our present day is
that of Wisdom. The Apostle Paul refers to Christ as God's Wisdom:
"We proclaim Christ crucified, a stumbling block to Jews and foolishness to Gentiles, but to those who are the called, both Jews and
Greeks, Christ the power of God and the Wisdom of God" (1 Cor
1:23–24).

The description of Wisdom in the eighth chapter of Proverbs parallels the description of Christ in the first chapter of Colossians. Wisdom existed before creation, was the first created Being, and was active in creation. Likewise Christ was "before all things," the "first-born of all creation," and the Creator of all things. The Gospel of John reveals Christ as "the way, and the truth, and the life" (Jn 14:6). Chapter four of Proverbs depicts Wisdom in similar terms as the path, the knowledge, and the way that insures life. The Hebrew word for "Wisdom" is *Hokmah*, and the Greek word for "Wisdom" is *Sophia*, both feminine nouns. This identification of Christ with feminine Wisdom reveals that the Christ who came into our world and who continually comes to us combines female and male, as well as humanity and deity, time and eternity. In the Bible, Sophia is a feminine image of Christ, just as Fatherhood is a masculine image of God.

We need the Advent of Christ-Sophia into our world today to bring wholeness to our worship and healing to our world. What ever happened to Christ-Sophia anyway? Why has She been so ignored in our Christian tradition? In all my years growing up, I never heard of Christ as Sophia. I never heard God referred to as "She," even though as we have seen in Proverbs, Wisdom is a biblical symbol for God, and Wisdom is "She." Throughout Christian history Christ-Sophia has been sadly missing. Our religion has been male-dominated, and feminine attributes of God have been overlooked or actively squelched. Instead of Wisdom, we have had wars; far too many of these have been religious wars. Instead of Wisdom, we have had injustice. Instead of the peace and cooperation that come with Wisdom, we have had hierarchy and greed. We have denied the full image of God and of ourselves, and things are all out of kilter. We need the coming of Christ-Sophia not just for fairness to females, but for the survival of creation. Without Christ-Sophia, we may all perish.

We need the Advent of Christ-Sophia to solve the massive problems that threaten our very survival. Ecologists tell us that we are rapidly using up our earth's resources, and that if we do not change our ways, our children will not be able to survive. We need Wisdom to know what to do to solve this problem. Similarly, we do not need sociologists or psychologists to tell us that racism continues to threaten our country, often in subtle but deadly ways. The average income of white Americans continues to be much higher than that of African-Americans and Mexican-Americans. We do not have to read statistics that women in our country still make only seventy cents to a man's dollar to know that sexism is still alive. Eighty percent of those in poverty are women and children. We are constantly bombarded with other problems that have no easy solutions: rising crime rate, AIDS, drug abuse, teenage pregnancy. On and on we can go with this list until we feel overwhelmed and depressed. We need Wisdom to come to us and help us find solutions to these problems that threaten our children, our youth, our elderly, and all of us in one way or another. Without Christ-Sophia, we will all perish.

Christ-Sophia will come to us if we are open and receptive. She is available to all—regardless of race, gender, or age. Christ, the Wisdom or Sophia of God, can come to us this Christmas even through the ways we choose to celebrate. Wisdom can lead us to simple, spiritual celebrations, ecologically and economically sound. Christ-Sophia can lead us away from commercial appeals to spend too much and waste too much. Wisdom can even lead us in the selection of toys for our children and grandchildren. So many toys labeled for boys teach aggression and violence, and those for girls teach excessive vanity and the need for male approval. When we buy these toys, are we contributing to the increase of the abuse of women through violence and pornography? Teaching boys that being a man means conquering, and teaching girls that being a woman means pleasing men leads to the abuse of females and an increase in violent deaths among both men and women.

Christ-Sophia can enable us to bring wholeness to our worship of God and wholeness to humankind. In a world of divisions and brokenness, wars and violence, we need the Advent of Christ-Sophia to bring wholeness. An exclusively masculine God encourages not only discrimination against women, but also racial and economic discrimination. Creating God in the image of a white-middle-class male supports the continued exclusion of a large portion of humankind from opportunity and power. Including the biblical image of Sophia in our image of Christ offers great potential for wholeness.

During this Advent season, our challenge is to consider ways in which we can participate in the coming of Christ as the Sophia, or Wisdom, of God. Christ-Sophia wants to come into our hearts. She calls to us and longs to show us the way. Just as Christ, the Sophia of God, called the first disciples, Christ-Sophia calls us to follow today. She calls to us. She stands at our gates. She cries out to us, "To you, I call. Learn from me. Acknowledge me. Spread my word." Christ-Sophia stands ready to come to us. She stands within our reach. She knocks at the doors of our hearts. We desperately need Wisdom to guide us, to change us, to bring justice and peace to our world. Wherever she comes, there is peace on earth, good will to all people.

Prayer for the Coming of Christ-Sophia

Christ, our Wisdom, why are you so far from us? Our world suffers from your absence. So few seek to be faithful to you. So few search for you. We, your children, want to find you and to bring your presence to our community. Show us the way. O Christ-Sophia, come to us! Teach us when to speak and when to be silent. Show us when to be cautious and when to forge ahead with your truth. Teach us when and how to confront falsehood. Guide us to change those things that diminish your creation. Teach us to speak and act in ways that affirm the worth of all your creation. Give us your vision for our community. May we follow your guidance in working toward your peace and justice. O Christ-Sophia, come to us! Amen.

EASTER: SEEKING THE RISEN CHRIST-SOPHIA

On Easter Sunday, the church proclaims the resurrection. We often make this amazing declaration in terms much more limiting than they need be. For instance, we sing, "Up from the grave He arose"; "He lives"; and "Christ the Lord is risen today, Alleluia! Sons of men and angels say, Alleluia!" Although words can never fully express the resurrection, these words place unnecessary limitations upon our experience of the mystery. This exclusively masculine language circumscribes the resurrection by time and gender. So many of our Easter hymns and litanies and sermons keep the risen One entombed in masculinity and in history. This contradiction has become so common that it is seldom even noticed.

Salvation cannot be restricted to reflection about the person and activity of the historical Jesus. It must deal primarily with the saving action that began with Easter and that continues until the eschaton.[3] The resurrection began in history with Jesus and moves to include all time and all creation. The invitation to resurrected life extends to all. Daughters, as well as sons, can then sing "Alleluia!" We can all rise from the grave because "She," as well as "He," has risen.

This Easter liturgy is intended to inspire faith as we continue to seek the resurrected Christ-Sophia and to find resurrected life for ourselves and our communities.

A Communal Search

(Congregation is seated in a circle with communion table in the center.)

All: Why have we come here? What are we looking for?

Reader 1:   (placing a large Bible on the communion table)
              I know why I'm here.
              I've come here for some answers.
              There're too many questions in the world today.
              I need to know what the Bible says.
              I'm here to find out exactly what God says.
              Because if God says it, I believe it, and that settles it.

All: Why are we here? What do we want?

Reader 2:   (placing a large pillow on the communion table)
              I'm here because I want to feel good.
              I listen to the news, and I feel bad.
              I work hard every day, and I feel tired.
              Even with my family I often feel frustrated.
              So this is one place I can come to feel good.
              I want to feel comfortable here.

All: Why did we come? Whom do we seek?

Reader 3:   (placing a superman figure on the communion table)
I'm here to find a big, strong Savior.
I want someone big enough to solve all my problems.
I need a superman to rescue me when I get in trouble.
There's too much evil out there for a meek and mild
      God.
I came to ask the Big Man Upstairs to wipe out the bad
      guys.

All: Why are we here? Whom do we seek?

Reader 4:   (placing a gold watch or a model of a BMW on the
      table)
I just want my share of the good life.
Coming here gets me near the One who can make me
      rich.
I want a God who gives me good things if I'm good.
There's nothing wrong with being rich and successful.
After all, money should be in the hands of good
      people.

All: Why did we come here? Whom do we seek?

Reader 5:   (placing a towel and a basin on the communion table)
There are so many things wrong with our world.
So many people suffer poverty and injustice.
I've experienced some of that myself.
I don't mean to sound pious or self-righteous.
But I'm seeking power for ministry.
I came here to gain faith and hope.
I came to find the One who sets the oppressed free.

All: Whom do we seek?
(all rising and joining hands)
We seek a risen Savior to bring us new life.
We need new life within and among us.

We seek Christ-Sophia,
Our wise and loving Savior,
The hope of all who seek Her,
The friend of all who find Her.
She Lives! Christ-Sophia lives today!

Meditation on Seeking
(based on John 20:1–16)

The setting is early one Sunday morning. A dark morning. A despairing morning. Mary Magdalene slowly makes her way to the grave. Her heart aches with grief and despair. Hopes dashed, the old demons creep back in, mocking her, "You thought you were really somebody. A disciple of the anointed One. Ha, ha, ha! All you are is a deluded woman. You thought this Jesus could change things for you. Now see what's happened. That's what happens to people who try to change things." Mary tries to close her ears to these voices, but terrible images keep flashing through her mind. Jesus hanging on a cross like a common criminal, crying out in agony, forsaken by everyone, even God. All Mary could do was stand helplessly by, watching, afraid to get too close. Perhaps she had been deluded all along. How could she have gotten her hopes up so high? She should have known that this message about God being on the side of the poor and the outcast was too good to be true. She should have known that this One who made her feel worthy and strong and capable could not last. This was just a fantasy. Now she would have to go back to the real world and her place in it: her place of powerlessness, of worthlessness. Demons of doubt, self-loathing, and hopelessness threaten to overwhelm her.

Mary Magdalene comes to the tomb and finds the stone taken away from the entrance. She runs and tells two of the other disciples. One looks and believes. But what does he believe? Whatever he has seen could not be for her to see as well, the demons keep saying. Mary stands weeping outside the tomb.

Through her grief comes a voice once and then again: "Woman, why are you weeping?" As she tries to pour out her grief, the question comes, "Whom do you seek?" The question comes from one she thinks is a gardener. This one standing beside her stops her protests by simply calling her name, "Mary." Suddenly in the echo of her name, she hears, she sees, she knows. Grief and despair turn to great joy. In that moment she knows she has found all she was seeking. Powerlessness and despair and death do not have the final word. New life and love and hope spring victorious. All is well! And all for her, most definitely for her. Mary responds to the miracle. She recognizes the resurrected Christ and responds as a disciple.

Like Mary Magdalene on Easter morning, we come haunted by demons of various shapes and sizes: demons of fear, of self-doubt, of egotism, of prejudice, of jealousy, of guilt, of apathy, of anxiety. We come with varying degrees of faith and hope. We come to hear or to see—something. We're not sure what. We've heard a tale of something better, something new and different, even miraculous. Is it true? Can we still hope? We come seeking something or Someone. Whom do we seek?

The one whom Mary hailed as "Teacher" had earlier said, "Ask, and it will be given you; seek, and you will find; knock, and the door will be opened for you" (Mt 7:7). Whom are we seeking? Our answer determines whom we find.

Throughout history people have sought a variety of saviors for a variety of reasons. In Jesus' day, people were looking for a messiah to support the nationalistic interests of Israel, to deliver them from Roman rule, to be a savior who would support the religious status quo and keep power in the hands of a few privileged males. They sought a Christ who would come dressed in military, royal splendor. They sought a warrior-king Christ.

This kind of Christ they did not find in Jesus of Nazareth. Jesus did not fit this image of the Christ they sought at all. Jesus came announcing God's favor upon those who had no chance in the present system of social status and religious tradition—the poor, the unclean, the unlearned, the despised lower classes of Palestinian society, the hated Samaritans, the women. Jesus did not come as a king and warrior, but as a suffering servant. Jesus came giving love and service to others, especially to the humiliated of society. Jesus taught a different kind of servanthood, a servanthood that was not simply acceptance of the servile status of the humble in the current society. Jesus demonstrated servanthood as a relationship to God that freed one from servitude to all human masters.[4] A revolutionary notion. Only a small group found Jesus to be the Christ—a despised Samaritan woman, a motley crew of twelve men who followed him around, Mary Magdalene, Joanna, Susanna, and many other women followers whom the writer of the Gospel of Luke did not think important enough even to mention by name. The rest found Jesus to be anything but the Christ. Jesus was not the one they were seeking at all. So they crucified him.

The small group who found Jesus to be the Christ continued to proclaim his message of good news to the poor and liberation for the oppressed. Transformed by the resurrection, they went forth boldly to transform individuals and unjust systems. Empowered by the Holy Spirit, they welcomed the gifts of all. Sons and daughters, and even female and male slaves preached (Acts 2:17–18). They made no distinctions between Jew and Gentile, slave and free, male and female; for they were all one in Christ Jesus (Gal 3:28). They shared their material possessions so that there was not a needy person among them (Acts 4:34).

Political and religious leaders continued to seek a Christ to support the status quo of power and privilege. Emperor Constantine used Christianity to justify the Roman political system. Constantine sought and created a Christ to sanction the status quo of slavery, sexism, and imperialism. He sought and created a Christ in the image of worldly lords and masters. Later theologians further established this kind of Christ. Thomas Aquinas in the Middle Ages said that neither slaves nor women could be priests because they could not image lordship and thus could not image Christ.

Prophets kept popping up, however, to remind us of another Christ, the Christ on the side of the poor and oppressed and disenfranchised. Julian of Norwich in the Middle Ages reminded us of a nurturing Mother Christ. St. Francis of Assisi reminded us of a Christ who joyfully takes the side of the poor. Sojourner Truth bucked the powers of church and state to preach a Christ who liberates us from slavery and sexism. Martin Luther King, Jr. reminded us of a Christ who challenges traditional religious and civil authorities by non-violent resistance to oppressive systems.

Whom do we seek? What kind of Christ do we seek? The Greek

verb "to seek" carries the meaning of "to study," or "to engage in the activities of a disciple." The Christ we seek will be the one we study, the one we follow. We can find support for a variety of Christs in Christian tradition. We may seek and find a Christ to support the politics of the privileged, to condone exploitation and oppression of the poor. We may seek a Christ to support a gospel of materialistic success. The popular song entitled "Jesus Wore a Rolex" satirizes those rich television preachers who wear flashy clothes, drive expensive cars, and live in luxurious houses. This materialistic gospel is widespread. We can even buy Christian designer jeans with the sign of the fish and the name "Jesus" stitched in golden thread on the hip pocket. A sign advertising these jeans reads "Witness with Style." Fund-raising consultants flock to the National Religious Broadcasting Convention to get their share of the lucrative business of religion. To them, spreading the message of Jesus is big business, selling everything from high-tech entertainment to coffee mugs and key chains promoting evangelists.

We may also seek a Christ who makes us feel comfortable in the status quo. Or we may seek a Christ who demands of us correct doctrine, but not transformed lifestyles. Whom do we seek? There are prophetic voices today reminding us of the Christ who stands in solidarity with the least of our sisters and brothers: the Christ who shows us what the reign of God looks like by standing on the side of those left out; the Christ whose resurrection brings not only individual salvation, but the salvation of oppressive systems and of the whole cosmos. Creation theologians and prophets seek a cosmic Christ who will save us from the destruction of God's creation, and bring spiritual awakening and justice. Liberation theologians and prophets seek a Christ who will free oppressed people. Feminist liberation theologians and prophets seek a Christ who saves us through the restoration of the male-female balance in God and in humanity.

We come seeking like Mary Magdalene on that first Easter Sunday morning. Waiting. Hoping. Seeking. Is it true? Is there resurrection? Is it for us?

The question of the resurrected One to Mary Magdalene rings down through the centuries to us: "Whom do you seek?" Our answer to this question is crucial. It determines whether or not we find new life and whether we bring new life to others and to all of creation. Do we seek One among the rich and the powerful? Do we seek Someone to support the religious and social status quo? Do we seek Someone to make us successful? Do we seek Someone among the dead or the living? Do we seek Someone among dead traditions, only in familiar forms? Or can we be open to the living, moving Spirit who transforms and creates new life?

The resurrected Christ came to Mary Magdalene in surprising form, more humble form than she was expecting. At first Mary did not even recognize the resurrected One. Christ still has a way of surprising us in unexpected forms and in unexpected places: in the face of a poor woman waiting in line at the Salvation Army shelter to receive food for her children; in the face of a homeless man shivering in a thin coat, lying under a bridge that provides little shelter from the cold wind; in the face of a young child dying of AIDS. Christ can still be found among the last and the least, the despised and rejected. When we seek the living Christ, we will find the One who conquered all the forces of sin and death to establish God's reign of shalom, the reign of justice and peace and well-being for all creation.

Adding the feminine to our language about Christ will help us to recognize Christ in our hurting sisters as well as brothers. Adding "She" to our language for Christ calls forth this recognition. Including the feminine dimension of Christ will help us find Wisdom to overcome oppressive systems. Biblical revelation links Christ and Wisdom, or "Sophia," in the original Greek language of the New Testament. Including "Sophia" in our language for Christ enlightens and empowers us for the work of justice. Calling Christ "She" and "Sophia" helps us to recognize Christ in the faces of poor women as well as men. Calling Christ "She" and "Sophia" helps us to recognize Christ in the bruised and bleeding face of a battered wife who fears she cannot survive if she leaves her abusive husband. Calling Christ "She" and "Sophia" helps us to recognize Christ in the face of the teenage girl who is pregnant for the third time because she has such low self-esteem that she cannot say "no" to boys.

Christ-Sophia calls us each by name. Christ-Sophia calls us to seek, to study, to follow the way of resurrection. We do not follow a dead teacher. We follow the way of resurrection and Wisdom. We follow a resurrected, dynamic, creative Teacher, who still proclaims, "See, I am making all things new" (Rev 21:5).

How can we believe in the resurrection when the world of hunger and poverty and injustice still exists? That world of injustice still exists because for too long we have sought the wrong kind of Christ in the wrong places.

Today the resurrection invites us to seek Christ-Sophia, to work toward the new creation, to imagine the new way. When we open ourselves to resurrection power, our imaginations are transformed. We see and believe in the new creation. We begin to act in the light and power of resurrection. We hope differently; we care differently; we eat differently; we act differently. We envision swords turned into plowshares, food and shelter and dignity for all, wholeness and beauty and laughter, all God's children becoming all God created each person to be. In the power of the resurrection, we can join with Christ-Sophia in bringing these visions into reality. In the power of the resurrection, we can join with Christ-Sophia in defeating evil and injustice. In the power of the resurrection, we can join Christ-Sophia in making all things new. Whom do we seek?

PENTECOST: RENEWING THE COMMUNITY OF CHRIST-SOPHIA

As we move through the sacred seasons of the year, we come to Pentecost. This day of celebration holds great power to renew faith communities. Unlike Christmas and Easter, Pentecost has remained free of commercialization in popular culture. Some traditions give Pentecost a prominent place, while others almost ignore it. All of us could experience revival through reclaiming the power of Pentecost.

With images of mighty wind and fiery tongues, Pentecost empowers communities to fulfill their missions. Peter's preaching of the Spirit's inclusiveness inspires the free exercise of gifts within communities. The miraculous outpouring of the Spirit on the day of Pentecost challenges people's faith to include the unexpected and the unplanned.

Pentecost is a most apt empowering symbol for inclusive worship communities. It clearly symbolizes the Spirit's continual activity in our midst. From the often seemingly miraculous, unplanned beginnings through the quiet miracles of overcoming obstacles to the growth that comes through many other victories and struggles, faith communities can experience surprise blessings not unlike those of the first Pentecost.

The following selections come from a Pentecost service intended to use the image of the Spirit of Christ-Sophia to breathe power into faith communities.

Call to Vision
(based on Habakkuk 2:2–3)

Leader: Make the vision plain,
            so that all may know and understand.

Voice 1:   Write the vision.

Voice 2:   Speak the vision.

Voice 3:   Sing the vision.

Voice 4:   Paint the vision.

Voice 5:   Act the vision.

Leader: Make the vision plain,
            so that all may know and understand.

All: The Spirit has poured out gifts upon all of us.
            Let us make the vision plain through our unique gifts.

(Members of the community give interpretations of their visions for the community through brief presentations, using gifts of word, song, art, or drama. After each presentation, the whole community stands and says, "You have made the vision plain. We embrace the vision.")

Leader: Our visions have their appointed time.
            If they seem slow in coming, we must wait.
            For they will surely come.

All: We have made our visions plain.
         We will act to make our visions a reality.
         And we will wait with faith and hope.
         For they will surely come.

Challenge to Keep the Dream Alive
(based on John 14:12)

Jesus left the disciples with this challenge and promise: "Very truly, I tell you, the one who believes in me will also do the works that I do and, in fact, will do greater works than these" (Jn 14:12). The disciples had harbored great dreams of the peace and healing that Jesus would bring to the world. They had even seen some of their dreams come true. Now Jesus was leaving them. They had just finished eating the Passover Feast, and Jesus was trying to tell them that this was their "Last Supper" together. Although they did not fully understand what he was saying, their hearts were heavy. In John chapter 14 we find Jesus' words of comfort. We also find these words of challenge to keep the dream alive.

Between the dream and its fulfillment lay doubt and fear and discouragement. Later we see the disciples waiting in an upper room in Jerusalem wondering what to make of all they had seen and felt. They went back to Jerusalem to wait, just as Jesus had told them. There they sat, in an upper room in Jerusalem, day after day, praying and waiting and waiting. Doubts plagued them. Maybe they had not really understood what Jesus had meant. How could they ever do the works that Jesus did and even greater works? Preposterous! They must have been crazy to have believed that they would actually do some of the miraculous things Jesus had done. Many people thought they were crazy for following this poor carpenter around and believing in miracles. And the resurrection — maybe that was all just wishful thinking. Could they prove the resurrection? So there they sat, waiting, doubting Jesus and themselves, but desperately holding on to the dream that Jesus had given them and wondering what they were supposed to do now.

Because they kept the dream alive, Jesus' promise to them became reality on the day of Pentecost. They received miraculous, life-changing power from the Holy Spirit! They began to speak differently, love differently, act differently. The Holy Spirit gave birth to the church on that day of Pentecost. The dream became a reality. The church began with a dream kept alive in the hearts of a few disciples.

The Holy Spirit continues to move with power and purpose, and to give birth to new communities. Today's new Christian communities are often intentional communities — gatherings of like-minded people seeking the living God and the Spirit of Christ-Sophia. Such communities can begin with a dream that the Spirit places in our hearts. Together we can battle doubts and resistance and discouragement. But the Spirit keeps moving with energy and urgency. The Spirit moves us to take that first step. To seize the moment. To claim the compelling message, to speak the vision into reality. The vision of women and men, black and white, standing side-by-side in ministry. The vision of women, as well as men, hearing themselves included in the language of worship. The vision of black as well as white children, girls as well as boys, becoming all God created them to be.

In grassroots inclusive worship communities we can witness the moving of the Holy Spirit — often in quiet, almost unnoticeable ways; sometimes in powerful, exciting ways. Even on those occasions when few members are present, the purpose and blessing of the Spirit remain in the community. Even when the group is far from its ideal of inclusiveness, it continues to affirm and reach toward its high calling.

The Spirit still moves to make all things new. The Spirit today urges us to keep our dream alive. To keep striving to make the vision of living, vibrant local Christian communities a reality. To keep our dream alive, we have to climb over some walls and jump on some springboards. The first wall we have to climb is the attitude that says, "What we're doing is all well and good, but not that important." We get this message directly and indirectly from others. They try to minimize what we're about by saying things like, "You're just too sensitive. Language in worship doesn't really matter. Changing a few words can't make that much difference. People don't really want racially integrated worship services. You're just a small group. What possible difference can you make?"

External voices often become internal walls. We doubt the importance of what we're doing and put it low in our priorities. We must climb over this attitudinal wall and reaffirm the urgency of our task. When two out of three of the poor in our country are women, and the majority of these are black and Hispanic, how can we ever doubt the urgency of our message? When eighty percent of the poor are women and children, and the majority of these are black and Hispanic, how can we ever question the seriousness of the mission to build inclusive communities based on the image of the Christ-Sophia? People all over the world are suffering and dying because of sexism and racism. Our mission is no less than the mission of Jesus: "To bring good news to the poor, proclaim release to the captives, let the oppressed go free" (Lk 4:18). Communities that embody these values are God-called and God-established to worship together, and to experience the power of the Holy Spirit to release the captives so that all God's children have the freedom to become all God created them to be.

The second wall we need to climb is the attitude that says, "We can't mix issues." Some think that we have to choose one issue: racial justice or gender justice. We can't work on both at the same time. This attitude assumes a limited supply of resources and a stinginess of spirit. The pie is only so big, and if one group gets a fair share, another group won't have enough. Some believe that we need to achieve racial equality before we work on gender equality. They worry that women are taking the few opportunities for minorities in leadership leaving Hispanics and African-Americans underrepresented. This attitude may explain the resistance of some black ministers to the ordination of women. We must climb over this attitudinal wall to discover the power of our unified efforts. We must shout with Dr. Martin Luther King, Jr.: "Injustice anywhere is a threat to justice everywhere!" When African-Americans suffer discrimination, all of us suffer. When women suffer discrimination, all of us suffer. The Holy Spirit urges us to unite and conquer the forces of oppression.

Another wall we must climb is the attitude that says, "Because we have not done everything, we have done nothing." This wall of discouragement and frustration blocks the power of the Holy Spirit. Too often we measure our success by society's standard of "bigger is better." We look at the size of our community, and it is not so big.

We reach out to bring change and meet resistance, indifference, and criticism. We can become discouraged, thinking our work is in vain. We have high ideals. We set out to change the world, and we wonder if we've even succeeded in making any changes within our own city, or even in our own families.

We must jump over this attitudinal wall by celebrating what we have accomplished. As a gymnast jumps on a springboard to gain the power to bound upward to reach the high goal, so God gives us springboards to reach the mark of our high calling. One of these springboards is the celebration of what we have accomplished. Our goal may still be way out there beyond our reach, but we see signs of victory in the experience of creative, inclusive services and the outreach that touches more people than we imagine.

The impact of the Spirit goes far beyond the community that welcomes the gift of the Spirit of Christ-Sophia. It carries far and wide through our involvement in other religious and civic organizations. We take into these different groups new insights and a greater sense of power in proclaiming these new insights. In one case the Holy Spirit brought change even from indirect contact with an inclusive worship community. A woman who teaches children's Christian education classes started using inclusive language and illustrations in her class. She had never attended an inclusive worship service, but became convinced that she needed to refer to God in this way through the witness of several people who had attended such services.

Another springboard that can lift us to higher accomplishments is the nurturing of our own community. As we strengthen and deepen relationships with one another, we gain power. As we come to understand one another better, we will be better able to unite and conquer the forces of oppression. We can gain courage for bolder endeavors through the acceptance and unity we feel in community. We can take courage in knowing that we are not alone. We are not just high-minded individuals striving toward self-fulfillment. We are a community of believers who have come together to take seriously Christ-Sophia's mission of liberating the oppressed. We can find strength by nurturing friendships within our community as we work toward a common mission. Let us begin today to celebrate what the Spirit is doing among and through us. Our celebration of achievement can become a springboard to lift us toward higher goals.

Another springboard to lift us upward toward our high goal is the affirmation of our vision. The prophet Habakkuk records these words of God: "Write the vision; make it plain on tablets, so that a runner may read it. For there is still a vision for the appointed time; it speaks of the end, and does not lie. If it seems to tarry, wait for it; it will surely come, it will not delay" (Hb 2:2–3). We must continue to make the vision plain, to lift the vision high before us, to believe that God will help us bring it to reality. Marie Curie's absolute confidence that she was discovering a new element kept her working through twelve years of formidable obstacles. She wrote her vision in her diary; she wrote that she had no doubt about the existence of the new element. But she was extremely handicapped by the lack of a proper place to work, lack of money, and lack of personnel. All she had for a laboratory was an abandoned shed with a glass roof that leaked when it rained. It was extremely hot in the summer and icy in the winter. Marie's health deteriorated from long hours and bad working conditions. But she believed so strongly in her vision of a new element that she would not give up. Four years of labor and eight tons of pitchblende finally yielded a tenth of a gram of radium, in the form of radium chloride. It took eight more years for her to isolate pure radium.[5] By holding on to her vision for twelve years, Madame Curie accomplished her goal. And because she did, we now have some of the miracles of modern medicine.

Christ-Sophia calls us to hold on to our vision, to continually affirm it. Christ-Sophia calls us to write the vision into reality. To speak the vision. To sing the vision. To act the vision. To love the vision into reality. Like the early disciples, we wait and pray for power from the Holy Spirit to keep our dream alive and make it reality. The Spirit will empower us to spring upward together toward the goal of our high calling. The Spirit gives us power to fulfill our mission which is Christ-Sophia's mission: "To bring good news to the poor, proclaim release to the captives, let the oppressed go free" (Lk 4:18).

Prayer for Renewed Vision

Spirit of the living Christ-Sophia, you have placed visions deep within our hearts. You have empowered us to take action toward the fulfillment of our visions. But we often hear voices of doubt and fear, and we become discouraged. We meet resistance and criticism, and we become frustrated. Our goals seem so high, and our resources so low. We wonder whether or not we're making any difference.

Spirit of all Power and Wisdom, we come to you today seeking the renewal of our visions. Breathe new winds of life into our dreams. Kindle new fires within our spirits. Give us faith to keep our visions alive and courage to make them a reality. Spirit of the living Christ-Sophia, fall fresh on us. Amen.

CHAPTER 9

Additional Worship Resources for Inclusive Communities

New worship resources become vital as individuals and communities progress from changes in their attitudes to changes in their actions. Many people resist this important transition from thinking to doing, keeping feminist theology on an intellectual level. We may feel more comfortable talking about the feminine divine images and the connections between Christ and Sophia in scripture than in making application to our worship practice. If we do not change our worship, however, these new insights remain lifeless. We begin to experience a frustrating dissonance between our beliefs and our actions, stifling the work of the Spirit in our lives.

With a biblical foundation for an inclusive christology firmly established, we can move with confidence toward implementation in our personal lives and religious communities. Essential to this process is the transformation of worship. We can begin by discovering ways to change familiar forms so as to infuse them with new meaning, such as the play on the words of the traditional Christmas carol "O Come, All Ye Faithful" in the Advent service in chapter eight above. New words to familiar hymn tunes can gently nudge us toward change. In this chapter, for example, the "Hymn in Celebration of Women's History Month" offers new words to the traditional hymn "For All the Saints." The surprise that comes from transforming familiar hymns and litanies awakens us to new spiritual possibilities.

The Spirit of Christ-Sophia also leads us to create new worship forms. At times we may follow a traditional pattern, such as the litany. In this chapter you will find litanies for the earth, for the celebration of woman as healer, for the praise of the Black Madonna, for Labor Day, and for many other occasions. As we continue to free the creative Spirit within us, we may break from familiar structures altogether.

When awakened to the importance of an inclusive christology, we may want to put our new insights into practice, but not know where to begin. The collection of resources in this chapter and in the preceding chapter represents one attempt to begin the implementation of an inclusive christology in worship. They are intended not only as a model of inclusive rituals, but as an impetus to the creativity of others.

These worship resources can be used in traditional church communities who understand the biblical basis for an inclusive christology and who want to put these insights into practice. By gradually introducing new hymns and litanies alongside the familiar ones, church members will grow in their openness to change. Many Christians, however, have become discouraged by the slowness of change in traditional churches and have formed alternative worship communities. These resources can serve as a ritual base for these alternative worship communities and a challenge to create new rituals. This collection is also intended to add to the store of worship aids for Women-Church groups. Although these aids have a communal format, individuals may also use them for personal prayer and meditation.

Ultimately, this collection of worship resources serves as an invitation to join the search for the resurrected Christ-Sophia through creating worship experiences that bring new life.

BIRTHING AN INCLUSIVE
WORSHIP COMMUNITY

This service contains excerpts from the inaugural service of the Inclusive Worship Community described in chapter seven. It connects the experience of bringing a diverse group of people together to birth a new community with the experience of those gathered on the day of Pentecost when the Spirit gave birth to the first church. Just as those early Christians felt the life-changing power of the Spirit, so the members of the new faith community experienced the Spirit's power to bring new life.

Responsive Call to New Life
(based on Acts 2 and Revelation 21:5)

Leader: When the day of Pentecost had come, they were all together in one place. And suddenly a sound came from heaven like the rush of a mighty wind, and it filled all the house where they were sitting. And there appeared to them tongues as of fire, distributed and resting on each one of them.

All: And they were all filled with the Holy Spirit And began to speak in other tongues.

Leader: They spoke with other tongues. The Spirit led them to speak words that reached people of many lands and races. The same Spirit moves today. This Spirit moves us to speak words that include all people. Listen! We no longer have to translate to feel included. We can hear the mighty works of God in our own tongues. Tongues that include women and men, black and white. Tongues of fire. Tongues of healing.

All: Behold, the spirit makes all things new.

Leader: Though some say we're full of new wine, we're not drunk. It's only 8:30 in the morning. We're not crazy. We just believe what God says, "I will pour out my Spirit upon all flesh, and your sons and your daughters shall prophesy, and your young shall see visions, and your old shall dream

dreams. Even upon my slaves, both men and
women, I will pour out my Spirit; and they shall
prophesy."

All: Behold, the Spirit makes all things new.

Leader: You can say that again!

All: Behold, the Spirit makes all things new.

Leader: Daughters preaching—that is a new thing! Age
             and race and class barriers broken down in the
             church—that is a new thing!

All: Behold, the Spirit is making all things new in
             Our very midst! For we are all filled with the
             Holy Spirit, and speak with new tongues.

Meditation on Revelation 21:1–6
by Sally Browder

Leader: I had a dream. I saw a new heaven and a new earth.
             The old world was no more. And I heard a loud voice
             saying:

Voice 1:   Behold, I make all things new.

Leader: I make all things neat. I make all things orderly,
             predictable. I am in control of my life, and I believe
             only what I can reason out. I do good things, of
             course, because I believe that this is how the world
             changes and is made right. I can take neither the
             miraculous nor the extremely evil seriously
             because it is out of my control. I arrange my world
             so I am not taken by surprise. But I am surprised,
             shaken, by the voice of the Spirit commanding:

Voice 2:   Behold, I make all things new.

Leader: I make all things part of the weight that bears me
             down. I ache at injustice around me and feel
             overwhelmed by it at times. Sometimes my anger
             and my frustration keep me from experiencing the
             good around me. What I do, I do self-consciously,
             aware of my limitations and weaknesses. I hunger
             for the word of hope and am encouraged and
             empowered by the voice of the Spirit affirming:

Voice 3:   Behold, I make all things new.

Leader: I make all things me versus them. I am not
             responsible for the way things are, but give me a
             moment, and I can tell you who is. And, if the truth
             be known, then were the righteous to parade into
             glory today, I would be near the front (not the very
             first perhaps, but neither the middle nor back). I
             don't boast about this; I merely know it in my heart.
             But, I am stunned, bewildered, (embarrassed?) and
             my pride is burned away by the inescapable voice of
             the Spirit observing quietly:

Voice 4:   Behold, I make all things new.

Leader: I had a dream. I saw a new heaven and a new earth.
             The old world was no more. Now is God dwelling
             among us. This is how it is to be God's people.
             And a voice says: "Write these words down
             because they are true and can be trusted.
             Indeed, it is already fulfilled."

The Hope and Challenge of New Life

We come today with a hope. A hope for change. We come today
with a challenge. A challenge to make our hopes reality. All of us

here this morning are prophets. We are prophets because we can imagine what is yet to be. We are prophets because we speak and act upon our hopes. We come together with prophetic hopes and visions.

Our hope is for women and men, black and white to stand side-by-side in ministry. Our hope is for our black children and our white children to sit side-by-side in church as well as in school. For female and male, black and white to share ministerial leadership. For women as well as men, black as well as white, to hear ourselves included in the language of worship. For our girls to learn that they are just as truly formed in the image of God as are our boys. For our black children as well as our white children, our girls as well as our boys, to become all God created them to be.

About a month ago, the Spirit began moving with unmistakable energy and urgency. The Spirit moved us to meet, and to say, "The time is right. We can delay no longer. Our message is too urgent. Our gifts are too precious. Our vision is too compelling."

We talked about waiting just one more month to begin, so that we would have more time for planning. It's always easier to delay, to wait for some more convenient time. But we could not quench the Spirit. Objections came up: it's too soon, it's Mother's Day, it's too near graduation. But this date kept insisting that it was the right time. So we took the leap of faith and scheduled this service for today. Last week during the planning process we discovered the reason. Today is Pentecost. Pentecost—that fire-filled day on which the Holy Spirit gave birth to the church. The Holy Spirit is leading us to begin a new work on this anniversary of that world-changing event. The timing is right. Now is the day of salvation. Now is the accepted time. This day in our very midst the Spirit is making all things new!

Our challenge today is to be open to the new work the Spirit is doing among us. The Spirit invites each one of us to participate. To follow Christ in working for justice and healing and reconciliation. To be a new community, not to fight existing institutions. To be a model and a light to the new direction of the Spirit in our day. The Spirit invites us to be a community which thrives on a great diversity of gifts and worship forms and leadership. A community which encourages creativity in all people—females and males of all ages, of all races, of all varieties of gifts. A community committed to inclusive actions and language, committed to avoiding all racism and sexism. Following Christ means resisting all racism and sexism for they are not of the Holy Spirit. We must maintain the integrity of our hope and vision by resisting sexist and racist language and actions. Our challenge is to speak the truth to one another in love, to help one another become aware of and eliminate racist and sexist language and actions.

Our challenge is to support one another in this new venture. We can be sure that we will meet criticism and obstacles and misunderstanding and belittling. Just as people made fun of the early Christians at Pentecost, saying, "They are filled with new wine" (Acts 2:13), there will be those who call us crazy or strange or unnecessary. There will be those who say that some of the things we stand for are only female issues or only black issues or only white issues. But we proclaim that they are human issues. When one suffers discrimination, we all suffer. When one group lacks opportunity, we are all impoverished. We are all diminished as human beings. But when women become free, men become free. When blacks become free, whites become free. The empowerment of one group becomes the empowerment of us all. The power of the Holy Spirit increases when shared. The Spirit gives power to all and makes all things new.

Today the Holy Spirit wants to fill us all so that we act in new ways and speak in new tongues. The wider community in which we all live desperately needs people who will speak in a different voice, a voice that affirms the gifts of all God's children, a voice that includes women as well as men, a voice that proclaims liberty for the oppressed, a voice that is indeed good news to the poor, a voice that calls for servant not authoritarian leaders, a voice of cooperation not competition in ministry, a voice of inclusion not exclusion. Let us seize this present crucial moment to proclaim God's transforming truth: "The Spirit makes all things new!" Just as the Holy Spirit gave birth to the church on that day of Pentecost almost two thousand years ago, the Spirit on this day of Pentecost is giving birth to something new.

Sisters and brothers, we hold in our hands the keys to a faith community that values the gifts of every member. We hold in our hands the keys to a community that models inclusiveness of gender and race, not just for fairness, but for the enrichment that comes with diverse gifts. The gifts of women and men, black and white are all manifestations of the Spirit. Hierarchies and segregations quench the Spirit. An inclusive community manifests the Spirit for the enrichment of all. It takes faith and hope to build a new community. We can encourage one another to keep faith and hope alive. And we can challenge one another to make our hopes reality.

We are all filled with the Holy Spirit. And behold, the Spirit makes all things new!

LITANY FOR THE EARTH
by Katie Cook[1]

Leader: God looked upon all the things that had been created
            —the sun, the moon and stars, the earth and all living
            things upon it,

All: And God said, "That's good!"

Leader: When we retreat into the wild places
            and surround ourselves with things God made,
            our spirits are healed,
            freed from the deafening noise that humans make.

All: We feel the stillness of a million summers,
            the peace that settles into our troubled hearts.
            We can hear the still, small voice of truth
            in the falling of a single leaf.
            And we say silently in our hearts, "That's good!"

Leader: When we see something naturally beautiful —
            a surprise splash of butterfly wings,
            the mystical, fleeting theophany of fireflies in the night,
            the majestic streak of brilliant color in the evening sky,

All: We feel the power and glory of God,

and we cry out with laughter
to the trees and clouds and insects —
"That's good!"

Leader: When we realize what we have done
to the planet God fashioned for us,
we feel anger and cynicism.

All: We point our fingers at each other and accuse,
for we cannot say that this is good.

Leader: Our word from God today is a hard saying.
It is that we have been unfaithful stewards.
We are the ones who clutter the earth with our refuse,
by clinging to our small comforts.

All: We have beaten our sister the earth
and left bruises and gashes;
we have raped her;
we have neglected her
and caused starvation and disease.

Leader: We have dabbled in her resources
and used them without adequate knowledge.
We have used them irresponsibly.
We have covered her face with our own masks.
Even now we hold a loaded gun to her head.

All: What can we do?
We long to once again hear God say, "This is good."

Leader: Our God is the Maker of second chances,
our God is the great Healer.
With God's help, we can make amends to our sister.
We can do small things to bind up her wounds.
We can restore her dignity.

All: With God's help, and with each other's support,

we can heal and nurture our sister the earth.
We now, before God, pledge to each other,
to God, and to the earth,
that we will again receive this precious gift,
and we will do all that we can to cherish it.

So that we all can say,
as God said in the beginning
about the earth and the heavens and all the living
creatures, "It is good."

SERVICE OF HEALING AND RENEWAL
FOR VICTIMS OF VIOLENCE
by Jean Batson Turner

Greeting

Leader: Peace be with you, and to all who enter into the presence of God.

All: Amen.

Words of Praise for God's Healing Power
(read by various members of the community)

Reader 1: "Restore us, O God! Let your face shine, that we may be
saved" (Psalm 80:3).

Reader 2: "In the shadow of your wings I will take refuge, until
the destroying storms pass by" (Psalm 57:1b).

Reader 3: "God remembers those who suffer; God does not forget
their cry" (Psalm 9:12a, adapted from NRSV).

Acknowledging the Pain

Leader: God of strength, the legacy of abuse is always with us. It twists itself around our spirits, choking out any sense of dignity or self-worth. It is an evil that binds our souls so that we are unable to believe that your love or mercy or compassion could be for us. Holy Spirit, sustainer of our lives and of our faith, be present with us by your grace. Empower us with your strength and courage that we may come to know ourselves as beloved of God, created, redeemed, and sanctified by the God who loves us with an everlasting love.

All: Amen.[2]

Sharing the Pain

Leader: We all share the pain of victimization. Many of us have borne particular hurts alone because society has silenced us, conditioning us to feel responsible for the violence inflicted upon us. We have endured abusive relationships and dehumanizing theology because the need to survive seemed more important than our total well-being. But now we choose to settle for nothing less than God's wish for us: complete physical, mental, emotional, and spiritual wholeness. Today, at this moment in this sacred place, we are gathered to share our common stories, as we press forward to God's new reign. You are invited now to name your particular pain.

            (Everyone is invited to share stories of pain and hurt.)

Leader: We now reaffirm our right to grieve for our losses. As our hurts are gathered up with the hurts of all our sisters and brothers, we will mourn silently for all those who have experienced violence.

            (Period of silent mourning.)

Leader: As our tears are mingled with God's tears, we somehow
            sense that new life is possible. We are not alone.

Assurance of God's Presence: Reclaiming the Promise
Paraphrase of the Twenty-Third Psalm (spoken in unison)

> The Lord is my friend!
> What more could I want?
> God sits with me in the quiet times of my days
> while exploring with me the meaning of life.
> God calls me forth as a whole person.
> Even though I walk along paths of pain,
> prejudice, hatred, depression,
> My fears are quieted,
> because God is with me.
> Through words and thoughts, I am challenged.
> God's spirit causes me to be sensitive
> to the needs of others.
> Then lifts up opportunities for serving.
> Such confidence stretches me.
> Surely love shall be mine to share throughout my life.
> And I shall be sustained by God's concern forever.[3]

Letting Go of Victimization (spoken in unison)

> I will no longer allow this experience of violence to dom-
> inate my life. I will not let it continue to make me feel
> bad about myself. I will not let it limit my ability to love
> and trust others in my life. I will not let my memory of
> the experience continue to victimize and control me.[4]

Ritual of Renewal and Self-Blessing
(Provide bowls of water.)

Group 1:   In blessing our foreheads... (all dip fingers in water and
            touch foreheads)

Group 2:   we claim the powers of reason.

Group 1:   In blessing our eyes... (all dip fingers in water and touch eyes)

Group 2:   we claim the power of vision, to see clearly the forces of life and death in our midst.

Group 1:   In blessing our lips... (all dip fingers in water and touch lips)

Group 2:   we claim the power to speak the truth about our experiences; we claim the power to name them.

Group 1:   In blessing our hands... (all dip hands in water)

Group 2:   we claim our powers as artisans of a new humanity.

Group 1:   In blessing our feet... (all dip fingers in water and touch feet)

Group 2:   we claim the power to walk the paths of our courageous foremothers, and when necessary, to forge new paths.

           (All join hands.)

All: In blessing one another, we claim the power that rests collectively in our shared struggle for justice.[5]

A Charge of Empowerment for New Life
(read by various members of the community)

Reader 1:   "We have escaped like a bird from the snare of the fowlers; the snare is broken, and we have escaped" (Psalm 124:7).

Reader 2:   "You have turned my mourning into dancing; you have taken off my sackcloth and clothed me with joy"(Psalm 30:11).

Reader 3:   "For it was you who formed my inward parts; you knit me together in my mother's womb. I praise you, for I am fearfully and wonderfully made. Wonderful are your works; that I know very well" (Psalm 139:13–14).

Reader 4:   "I have calmed and quieted my soul, like a weaned child with its mother; my soul is like the weaned child that is with me" (Psalm 131:2).

Reader 5:   God "is my light and my salvation; whom shall I fear?" (Psalm 27:1a).

Reader 6:   "Do not forsake Wisdom, and She will keep you safe; love Her, and She will guard you" (Proverbs 4:6, adapted from NRSV).

Blessing for Dismissal
(spoken in unison)

> May our Sister God, who held us at our birth, who
> stands beside us in our joy and our grief, and
> who gathers us up into her life-giving embrace,
> be with us, now and always. Amen.[6]

PRAYER FOR RELEASE FROM OPPRESSION
by Nancy Ellett Allison

All: We approach you today, O Nourishing God, as people often parched from a dry and desperate past.

Leader: A past where our minds

Circle 1:   have grown doubtful through ridicule and questioning, have not been valued for our intuitive leaps, have grown weary trying to discern "the right way."

All: We reach out to you today, O Loving God, with arms that ache to be embraced.

Leader: For in the past our bodies

Circle 2:   have been enslaved by persons and structures,
            have been devalued for their life-giving cycles,
            have been abused by those who met their needs through
            our innocence.

All: We search for you today, O Mysterious God, with spirits
            yearning to find expression in this world.

Leader: For in past ages our spirits

Circle 3:   have been crushed for their enthusiasm,
            have been stifled by decree and dictum,
            have been shackled by oppression.

All: In the past, O Nourishing, Loving, Mysterious God, our
            minds, our bodies, our spirits have been reviled by those
            who did not see us as creatures created in your image.
            Our minds, our bodies, our spirits have not been valued
            as expressions of your glorious nature.

            Release us today, Empowering God, from hostility for
            these actions against us, and our sisters and brothers. As
            we forgive our offenders, may you forgive them as well,
            so that we might be free to bring the fullness of our-
            selves—our integrated spirit, body, and mind—into this
            ever-changing present!

CONFESSION OF COMPLIANCE
WITH OPPRESSION AND
CLAIMING OF POWER FOR CHANGE
by Jann Aldredge-Clanton

Leader: We have not trusted our deepest yearnings.

Circle 1:   Now Faith revives us to fulfill our inmost call.

Leader: We have not embraced the bounty of our bodies.

Circle 2:   Now Beauty beckons us to cherish and nourish ourselves.

Leader: We have not proclaimed the visions of our spirits.

Circle 3:   Now Hope inspires us to birth our dreams.

Leader: We have not developed the full potential of our minds.

Circle 1:   Now Wisdom enlightens us to become creators of a new world.

Leader: We have not claimed the fullness and diversity of our talents.

Circle 2:   Now Love empowers us to celebrate and nurture all our gifts.

Leader: We have not asserted our power and freedom as healers.

Circle 3:   Now Truth sets us free to lead the way to wholeness.

All: Giver of all good gifts,
            Revive us with your Faith,
            Nourish us with your Beauty,
            Inspire us with your Hope,
            Enlighten us with your Wisdom,
            Empower us with your Love,
            Lead us by your Truth to become the
            Healers you created us to be. Amen.

PRAYER OF EMPOWERMENT FOR HEALERS
by Nancy Ellett Allison

All: Take our hands, Creator of the Universe, and cause us to be creative as well.

Leader: As we touch, may we feel the need within others,

Circle 1: And may the ones we touch feel our care.

Leader: As we touch, may we feel the pain within others,

Circle 2: And may the ones we touch know understanding and experience peace.

Leader: As we touch, may we feel the disorder within others,

Circle 3: And may the ones we touch be reshaped and restored to wholeness.

All: Take our minds, Spirit of Wisdom, and cause us to be wise as you are wise.

Leader: As we work, may our minds be quick to see connections between despair and illness, hope and wholeness.

Circle 1: As we watch, may our minds be challenged to see the truth and not just what we expect to see.

Leader: As we wait, may our minds be filled with your strength and your grace, your vision and your presence, your joy and your sorrow,

Circle 2: So that healing may flow from all that is within us to all whom we touch.

All: Take our lives, O Spirit Divine, and expand us with your breath so that we may continue to grow toward all you created us to be.

LITANY IN CELEBRATION
OF WOMAN AS HEALER
by Dawn Darwin and Tracy Dunn-Noland

Voice 1: (read by an older woman)

I AM

Woman remembered in the twilight glow,
Overcoming odds few can know,
Making new ways for my path to go.
Am I certain this calling is worth the cost?
Nothing is waiting to replace what I've lost.

Ambushed by a world in pain,
Sophia's gentle wisdom beckons me again.

Hear the voice of the One who stirs me,
Enter her dance with its saving plea.
A path is emerging for Spirit-followers to see,
Leading to refuges of healing and peace.
Even if only for a moment or three,
Return to God's dream of how whole the world can be.

All: My mother's voice! I know it well.
Her story I will boldly tell.
Her healing touch will always be,
For she is a part of me.

Voice 2: (read by a middle-aged woman)

I AM

Woman seen in the noonday sun,
Overcome by the heat of what has scarcely begun!
Making ends meet can become
A poor substitute for friendship, fulfillment, and fun.
No is a word seldom heard on the run.

Absorbed in the crossfire between now and not yet,
Sophia's gentle wisdom can be easy to forget.

Hurled from chore to chore,
Easily succumbing to guilt for not doing more,
Aptly I balance my anger and hopes, fighting a holy
     war,
Leaning to any side I find all around me a web is cast,
Eager to hold me in connectedness in which I can bask,
     that I may
Reach the prize while I soar!

All: My sister's voice! I know it well.
          Her story I will boldly tell.
          Her healing touch will always be,
          For she is a part of me.

Voice 3: (read by a young girl)

   I AM

   Woman glimpsed in the day's first rays, I am
   Overwhelmed in joy, singing God's praise!
   Mother, I cry, we've come through the haze of
   Anguishingly, slowly changing days.
   New life does come from the grave!

   A new day has dawned and the walkway is clear,
   Sophia's gentle wisdom has torn down walls with our
        cheers.

   Hope is not a distant dream.
   Every corner is filled with reason to sing!
   A woman, a world is born.
   Let the bells of healing ring!
   Each morning I grow in awareness of the gifts that I
        bring.
   Rejoice! The Spirit is creating new things!

All: My daughter's voice! I know it well.
          Her story I will boldly tell.
          Her healing touch will always be,
          For she is a part of me.

ADVENT DRAMA:
WHO'S THAT IN THE MANGER?
by Sally Browder

This drama can be performed as a playlet or reader's theater program during an Advent worship service.

Characters: Five teenagers (two male, three female) and a narrator.

Scene: It is the Advent season and the youth group is preparing for a Christmas program. A teenage boy named Peter is busily putting up Christmas decorations, hanging greenery around the stage and ornaments on the Christmas tree. Two teenage girls, Susanna and Joanna, and a boy named John enter carrying a large cardboard or wooden manger. An unnamed pregnant teenager enters as noted in the script. A narrator offers a concluding reflection.

Susanna: We better set up this manger.

John: Where does it go?

Peter: How about over here?

Joanna: No, I think here would be better.

Peter: Go ahead and put it wherever you want to. I'm working on the decorations. (continues decorating the stage)

           (The others busy themselves setting up the manger. A girl around fourteen-years-old, with pillow stuffed under her dress so that she looks pregnant, enters quietly and stands near Susanna.)

Susanna: (to the girl) Excuse me. Would you mind not getting in the way?

John: Hey, isn't that Anne's kid?

Joanna: Aren't you Anne's child? Why, I know your family. What happened to you?!

Susanna: (to John) She must be such a disappointment to her family.

John: (to Susanna) Wonder where she went wrong.

Peter: Are you here to help?

Joanna: How could she help, in her condition!

            (All laugh.)

Susanna: (to girl) Can't you see we're busy? Excuse me! (moves her out of the way)

John: Are you here to help?

Peter: (pulling girl aside) Look, let me tell you. We've got some important preparations going on here. We just really don't have room for you to hang around.

Susanna, John,
and Joanna: (mumbling) No room, no room, no room...

Joanna: (to girl, as she walks slowly off stage) Maybe, if you were here to help...

            (All finish up their work.)

Susanna: Well, what do we do now?

John: What do we do now?

Peter: I wonder why somebody doesn't come.

Joanna: We're ready.

Susanna: Yeah, why doesn't someone come?

John: Well, maybe we could wait over here where it's comfortable.

Peter: Well, I don't know about you all, but I've got some Christmas shopping to do.

Joanna: Me too. Where's my list?

Peter and
Joanna: (walking off stage together) Don't you love this time of year?

Susanna
and John: (following them off stage and mumbling) No room, no room...

               (Girl re-enters.)

Girl: Do you have to treat me like I am a criminal? You know me. I see you in school. We are in class together. You know my family. But now you ignore me or look down your noses at me. Or say I got what I deserve. Or you are glad you are not me. I wish I were not me. Why me, God? If there is a God. I wanted to be loved. I've always wanted to be loved. Is that so bad? He said he loved me. So, betrayed with a kiss. I feel so ugly. So unwanted. There are things I wanted to do with my life. I had plans, but I don't think I'm really smart enough, and who would take care of the baby anyway. It feels like my life is over before it even began.

(Girl climbs in manger and curls up to sleep.)

Narrator: She was despised and rejected by others; one who knew suffering and was acquainted with grief; and as one from whom others hide their faces she was despised, and we held her of no account. Surely she has borne our griefs and carried our sorrows; yet we accounted her stricken, struck down by God, and afflicted. But she was wounded for our transgressions, she was crushed for our iniquities; upon her was the punishment that made us whole, and by her bruises we are healed. (adapted from Isaiah 53:3-5)

(Susanna, John, Peter, and Joanna re-enter.)

Susanna: Hey! Who's that in the manger?

(Freeze this scene, while congregation sings "Child in the Manger.")

Concluding Song: *Child in the Manger*

Child in the manger, Child full of sorrow,
Outcast and stranger, bearing disgrace,
Can our salvation rest in your suffering,
Hope of creation in this low place.

Child in the manger, help us to learn to
welcome the stranger, holy embrace.
Love those who wrong us, serve those who scorn us,
Christ Child among us, bring us to grace.[7]

LITANY OF PRAISE
FOR THE BLACK MADONNA
adapted by Robert L. Uzzel

Leader: Like some long unremembered ancient lore
            Pushed carelessly aside, I find you here
            Unnoticed in the little modest niche
            Of an art gallery's cluttered basement drear.

All: Oh Black Madonna, what hand carved this face
            With saintly beauty etched in every line,
            What inspired artist gave to you the grace
            That speaks of love both tender and sublime?

Leader: Were you the ancient mother of a god
            Worshiped by folk when worlds were young and new;
            And did you bear beneath that fulsome breast
            A martyr son of the same ebon hue?

All: Oh Black Madonna, what hand carved this face
            With saintly beauty etched in every line,
            What inspired artist gave to you the grace
            That speaks of love both tender and sublime?

Leader: Today I find you in this unmarked place
            And in my heart I resurrect your shrine.

All: Oh Black Madonna, what hand carved this face
            With saintly beauty etched in every line,
            What inspired artist gave to you the grace
            That speaks of love both tender and sublime?[8]

HYMN IN CELEBRATION
OF WOMEN'S HISTORY MONTH
adapted by Sally Browder

For all the saints who from their labor rest,
Who thee by faith before the world confessed,
Thy name, O Jesus, be forever blest.
Alleluia, Alleluia.

Thou wast companion in their joy and pain;
Thy presence proof their work was not in vain.
Thou, Mother Christ, to hope gave birth again.
Alleluia, Alleluia.

O may we join these sisters from before,
Speak as one voice, define one holy chore.
Take up the call for justice evermore.
Alleluia, Alleluia.

And when we falter from our labor long,
Share with us still thy shining grace-full song,
That hearts are brave again and voices strong.
Alleluia, Alleluia.[9]

MOTHER'S DAY SERVICE
by Jann Aldredge-Clanton

Call to Worship (based on Genesis 1)

Leader: In the beginning God gave birth to the universe.

All: God gave birth to light. And God said, "That's good!"

Leader: God gave birth to the earth, and God saw that it was
            good.

All: God gave birth to the grass and trees and plants
            of all kinds, and said, "That's good!"

Leader: God gave birth to cattle and all kinds of animals, and
            saw how good they were.

All: Then God gave birth to female and male in God's own
            image. And God said, "That's good!"

Leader: And God blessed female and male with responsibility
            for the earth and all the living things that She had
            birthed.

All: We come to celebrate these gifts from God and to
            learn again what it means to be entrusted with them.

Hymn of Praise: *This is My Mother's World*

> This is my Mother's world,
> And to my list'ning ears,
> All nature sings, and round me rings
> The music of the spheres.
> This is my Mother's world,
> I rest me in the thought
> Of rocks and trees, of skies and seas;
> Her hand the wonders wrought.
>
> This is my Mother's world,
> The birds their carols raise;
> The morning light, the lily white
> Declare their Maker's praise.
> This is my Mother's world,
> She shines in all that's fair;
> In the rustling grass I hear Her pass,
> She speaks to me ev'rywhere.
>
> This is my Mother's world,
> O let me ne'er forget

That though the wrong seems oft so strong,
She is the Ruler yet.
This is my Mother's world,
The battle is not done;
Jesus who died shall be satisfied,
And earth and heaven be one.[10]

Prayer of Petition

All: God, our Mother, you continually give life to us.
          Nourish us and teach us to become all you created us to
          be. Help us to receive your tenderness and respond to
          your challenge so that others may draw life from us.
          Amen.

Hymn of Celebration: *Faith of Our Mothers*

Faith of our mothers living still
In spite of dungeon, fire, and sword,
O how our hearts beat high with joy
Whene'er we hear that glorious word!
Faith of our mothers, holy faith!
We will be true to thee till death.

Faith of our mothers leads us to Thee,
O God, our Mother, unto Thee.
O may the truth that comes from Thee
Make us all just and truly free.
Faith in our Mother, holy faith!
May we be true to Thee till death.[11]

Scripture Reading

As an eagle stirs up her nest,
flutters over her young,
spreads abroad her wings,
takes them, bears them on her wings:
So God alone did lead them,

and there was no strange god with them.
(Deuteronomy 32:11–12, adapted from KJV)

Hymn of Preparation: *Jesus, Savior, Pilot Me*

Jesus, Savior, pilot me
Over life's tempestuous sea;
Unknown waves before me roll,
Hiding rock and treach'rous shoal;
Chart and compass came from Thee:
Jesus, Savior, pilot me.

As a mother stills her child,
Thou canst hush the ocean wild;
Boist'rous waves obey Thy will
When Thou say'st to them, "Be still";
Wondrous Sov'reign of the sea,
Jesus, Savior, pilot me.[12]

Reflections on the "Ideal Mother"

Our first child was born in June. For over a year he had colic and other digestive problems. It seemed that he cried constantly. Before he was born, I had read all kinds of books on child psychology and development: books like *How to Give Your Child a Superior Mind,* which told what to do from the first day on. You see, I wanted to be the perfect mother. But that first year I had no energy or time to give my child a superior mind; satisfying his basic physical needs seemed to take all our time. I remember those long, sleepless nights, rocking him while he cried. I felt so inadequate as a mother. What was I doing wrong?

The next May I looked forward to my first Mother's Day. By that time I felt I deserved a little recognition for all my struggles. I went to church, hoping to hear words of help and hope. But instead, what I heard from the preacher made me feel more inadequate and guilty. He kept talking about how God wanted mothers to be self-sacrificing, patient, self-denying in our love for our children. He painted the portrait of the ideal mother. This ideal seemed impossible for me to reach. I had come for words of hope and strength, but left feeling hopeless and powerless. Words of a song I had learned as a child kept going through my mind:

> 'M' is for the million things she gave you;
> 'O' means only that she's growing old;
> 'T' is for the tears she shed to save you;
> 'H' is for her heart of purest gold;
> 'E' is for her eyes of love light shining;
> 'R' means right and right she'll always be.
> Put them all together they spell 'MOTHER,'
> A word that means the world to me.

It was not until much later that I realized that the Mother's Day sermons and songs held up an ideal of motherhood impossible for any mortal mother to achieve. Religious and secular institutions both held up a superhuman image of a mother: "'T' is for the tears she shed to *save* you....'R' means right and *right she'll always be.*" These words could not possibly describe a human being! This description is of no less a being than God. The ideal we have held up for mothers is a superhuman, impossible ideal for any human being. Only God could be this Ideal Mother.

We have expected mothers to be like God, but without the advantage of any female divine images. The church has left mothers totally bereft of a Divine Mother from whom we can draw strength, or who can take over for us when we feel weak and inadequate. What the church has done spiritually and psychologically for fathers, it has denied to mothers. Our churches constantly undergird fathers with images of God as Father. This provides a powerful kind of support for fathers in their task. They can feel a kind of identity with a strong Father God, who strengthens them for their fathering tasks, takes up the slack, makes up for their weaknesses and limitations. But we leave mothers to go it alone. The absence of a Mother God image is a spiritual and emotional injustice to mothers and their children, as well as to fathers, who could benefit from an equally strong partner in the parenting task. In addition, it is biblical and theological heresy.

We have ignored the powerful images of God as Mother in scripture. God is indeed the Ideal Mother. The first chapter of Genesis pictures God as a Mother giving birth to the universe. "In the beginning God created the heavens and the earth. The earth was without form and void, and darkness was upon the face of the deep; and the Spirit of God was moving over the face of the waters" (Gen 1:1–2, RSV). The Hebrew word for Spirit (*ruah*) is feminine. The word translated "moving" (*rachaph*) also means "flutter over" and is used only one other time in the Bible to describe God's action: Deuteronomy 32:11 which compares God to a mother eagle fluttering over her young. Thus we see that the very first picture of God in the Bible is that of a Mother Spirit giving birth to creation.

As we follow the history of Israel, we see God continuing as a loving Mother, nurturing and guiding her children. In a key passage in Exodus, God renews the covenant with Israel. Although the people had been unfaithful to God, she offers another chance: "I will be gracious to whom I will be gracious, and will show mercy on whom I will show mercy" (Ex 33:19). The Hebrew word (*rahum*) translated "mercy" is literally translated "womb-love."[13] This passage pictures God as a Mother who continually loves and forgives the children of her womb.

In the Book of Deuteronomy we find the strong, tender image of God as a mother eagle: "As an eagle stirs up her nest, flutters over her young, spreads abroad her wings, takes them, bears them on her wings: So God alone did lead them, and there was no strange god with them" (Dt 32:11, adapted from KJV). The mother eagle stirs up her nest when it is time to get her young out on their own. She takes them on her wings to show them how to fly. Then when she thinks they are ready, she swoops down to let them fly on their own. But she stays close enough to swoop back under them when they become too weary and weak to continue to fly alone.[14]

This picture of God as a mother eagle helps us to understand God as nurturing and supporting us when we are weak, yet always encouraging us to grow and mature. This divine image models for us a non-possessive maternal love.

One of the most beautiful pictures of God's love and care is that of a comforting Mother God: "As a mother comforts her child, so I will comfort you; you shall be comforted in Jerusalem" (Is 66:13).

Just as the exiled Israelites could feel comfort from this assurance of a tender Mother God, so we can feel the comforting arms of Mother God in our times of distress.

The New Testament continues these images of God as a gracious Mother, who longs for the best for her children. Jesus cries out, "Jerusalem, Jerusalem, the city that kills the prophets and stones those who are sent to it! How often have I desired to gather your children together as a hen gathers her brood under her wings, and you were not willing!" (Mt 23:37). The Spirit of God who fluttered over the waters to bring forth creation is the same God who in Jesus longs to re-create us under her loving wings. Jesus yearns to be the loving Mother who gives the best to her children.

The image of the new birth is central to biblical revelation. Jesus tells Nicodemus: "No one can see the kingdom of God without being born from above....What is born of the flesh is flesh, and what is born of the Spirit is spirit" (Jn 3:3,6).

The image of a mother bringing forth life presents a unifying picture of God throughout the Bible. In the first chapter of Genesis, we see the Spirit (female _ruah_) giving birth to all creation. After humanity breaks the covenant with God, the Spirit gives birth to new creatures through the Christ-Sophia. The picture of God as Mother giving birth links creation and redemption.

Calling God "Mother" restores the original balance of creation. When we call God "Mother," we are not saying that God is only female, for we know that God includes feminine and masculine and much more. But calling God "Mother" provides a much-needed image for the wholeness of the human race and the survival of the earth. When we call God "Mother," we give human mothers that divine support needed for parenting. Calling God "Mother" helps us to feel more fully the nurturing and gentle, as well as the strong and protective, qualities of God. Calling God "Mother" empowers us to fulfill our sacred duty of preserving all creation which God birthed. Only God can be the "Ideal Mother."

Doxology and Benediction

> Praise God from whom all blessings flow,
> Praise Her all creatures here below,

Praise Her above ye heavenly host.
Praise Mother, Christ, and Holy Ghost.[15]

LITANY FOR LABOR DAY
by Sally Browder

Call to Worship

Group 1:   We come, we who labor and are weighed
             down with responsibility, uncertainty, and worry.

Group 2:   We come, because the load we carry is heavier
             than we can bear alone.

Group 1:   We come, seeking to relate work and worship,
             leisure and service, into a meaningful whole.

Group 2:   We come, needing to share our burdens, and
             hoping to find God's comfort and strength
             through this community.

Group 1:   We gather for spiritual renewal and practical
             challenge, for help in making choices and
             carrying out commitments.

Group 2:   We come, sinners and saints, with our hatreds
             and loves, our failures and successes, our
             sorrows and joys.

All: We respond to the Spirit's leading and open
             ourselves to receive God's gracious gifts.[16]

Prayer for All People

Leader: Living God, we pray for all people:

             (Individuals should read the following lines silently,

and then offer aloud the lines they wish to pray.)

Individuals:

For those women shut off from a full life by tradition and practice.

For those people who are oppressed and exploited.

For those denied their freedom and dignity by systems and authorities.

For those forced to leave their homelands because of their beliefs.

For those seeking answers and meaning to their lives within their own cultures and religions.

For those who labor too long and too hard yet can barely feed and clothe themselves and their families.

For those forced to sell their bodies to survive.

For those women and men who live lives of quiet desperation at the hands of the powerful and prestigious.

Leader: For these and all who suffer, we pray, asking that this community may give joyful expression to your creative love, which breaks down barriers and unites person to person, woman to man, and community to community. This gives meaning and hope to empty lives, and makes us reach out to one another in generous self-giving, which makes us more complete ourselves.

All: So God, fulfill your promise in us for the sake of all human beings. Amen.[17]

Closing Blessing

Group 1:   God gives life.

Group 2:   God renews life.

Group 1:   Celebrate the life within you and within this
            community. Let it overflow to enliven the world.

Group 2:   May the peace of God dwell within you this
            week and forevermore.

All: AMEN!

LITANY FOR ANY OCCASION
by Jann Aldredge-Clanton

Call to Worship

Leader: O come, let us worship God, our Mother and Father.
            Let us worship Christ-Sophia, our Sister and
            Brother. Let us worship the Spirit, our Comforter
            and Guide.

All: To worship is to glorify God's name, to dance with
            the Spirit, who is alive in each of us.

Leader: To worship is to open ourselves to new revelations,
            to new truth from Christ-Sophia, our Wisdom.

All: Before all other things Wisdom was created. In
            each generation Wisdom passes into holy souls.
            She empowers us to be her prophets of
            peace and justice.

            Christ-Sophia, our Wisdom, come to us. Give

us new visions. Set us free to be your new creation.
Amen.

Affirmation of Faith

Leader: Let us affirm our faith together.

All: We believe in the living God who gave birth to us,
            the God who is Mother and Father, Sister and
            Brother, She and He, Black and Brown and White,
            and so much more than we can ever imagine. We
            believe that this God became flesh in Jesus, who
            rose from the dead and now lives as sisters and
            brothers who are united in loving community. As this
            resurrected Body of Christ-Sophia, we proclaim
            good news to the poor, heal the brokenhearted, and
            liberate the oppressed. God continually calls us to
            join Her as co-creators of justice, beauty, and
            peace. We accept this calling with the confident
            expectation of the final completion of God's purposes.

Responsive Meditation

Leader: What good is the gold that gilds the affluent
            and supports a two-tier system in religion and in
            the world?

All: Follow Christ-Sophia, who is simple and poor
            and politically unencumbered.

Leader: What good is the incense that burns with a flair
            on the altars of our own making?

All: Follow Christ-Sophia, the Spirit of Wisdom
            and Love and Truth.

Leader: What good is the myrrh that masks the pain
            and embalms our dead intentions?

All: Follow Christ-Sophia, who died and rose
            from the symbols of decay.

Leader: You will hear sage advice
            about overpowering others.

All: Rather be overpowered
            by that power pressed to a cross.

Leader: Wise are the ones who hear this word
            and do their best to keep it.

All: Wise are the daughters and sons of Christ-Sophia,
            for they hold these things in their hearts.[18]

THE 23rd PSALM
adapted by Bobby McFerrin

This piece of music is suitable for meditation and for deepening the
experience of God's presence. Play the music and then ask members
of the community to talk about their feelings. The words are powerful in themselves but the musical score is needed to experience
the full impact.

> The Lord is my Shepherd,
>   I have all I need.
> She makes me lie down in green meadows,
>   beside the still water She will lead.
> She restores my soul;
>   She rights my wrongs.
> She leads me in a path of good things,
>   and fills my heart with songs.
> Even though I walk through a dark and dreary land,
>   there is nothing that can shake me;
> She has said She won't forsake me,
>   I'm in Her hand.
> She sets a table before me

in the presence of my foes.
She anoints my head with oil,
    and my cup overflows.
Surely, surely goodness and kindness will follow me
    all the days of my life.
And I will live in Her house forever,
    Forever and ever.
Glory be to our Mother, and Daughter,
    and to the Holy of Holies.
As it was in the beginning,
    is now and ever shall be,
World without end, Amen.[19]

One man responded to this song with deep emotion. He said that he had never had such a profound feeling of God's acceptance and of being totally surrounded by love and care. The feminine language opened up for him a fuller experience of God and a greater acceptance of himself.

A clergywoman expressed the feeling of being understood and empowered by God in a deeper way than ever before. This woman had felt betrayed by her denomination which had encouraged her to follow God's call and then had denied her vocational opportunities because of her gender. She said, "The image of God as a 'She' who 'rights my wrongs' makes me feel that God understands and works with me to heal discrimination against women. Thinking of God as a 'She' helps me to claim my own creativity and power for righting wrongs."

One man recalled images of his grandmother's tender, nurturing love: "I felt so peaceful and content as I listened to the song, just as I remember feeling when my grandmother held me in her lap and rocked me."

One woman expressed overwhelming feelings of comfort and peace, and another said she felt as though God were carrying her through the difficult times she was experiencing.

One member of the community felt more comfort from this version of the 23rd Psalm than from the traditional version: "The images in the Bobby McFerrin song felt more uplifting and reassuring, and the feminine language seemed more natural."

Conclusion

While some feminist theologies exalt the image of the goddess as an alternative to the exclusively masculine image of God that is common in traditional Judaism and Christianity, this book has put forth the image of Christ-Sophia. Christ-Sophia holds the promise of liberation and redemption that is central to biblical revelation and Judaeo-Christian faith. The image of the goddess, like traditional images of a male god, offers a symbolism limited to one gender. The image of Christ-Sophia provides a holistic, egalitarian symbolism, and invites discovery of a new egalitarian theology and worship. Christ-Sophia focuses on the resurrection of a holistic divine image and provides a foundation for an inclusive faith community. Patriarchal Christianity must die for this resurrection to take place: "Unless a grain of wheat falls into the earth and dies, it remains just a single grain; but if it dies, it bears much fruit" (Jn 12:24). As the single grain of masculine christology dies, an inclusive christology springs forth to bear much fruit.

At a time in history when destruction threatens our connections with one another and with the earth itself, Christ-Sophia brings us hope. Christ-Sophia symbolizes the integration of feminine and masculine, of black and white, of human and divine, of body and spirit, of immanence and transcendence. By becoming incarnate as a human being, Christ-Sophia bridges the gap between Creator and creation. Christ-Sophia, by becoming one with the earth through incarnation and suffering, corrects the tendency to identify the transcendent with the male and the immanent with the female. The image of Christ-Sophia also makes us aware of our own collective power as co-creators of the earth.

Jesus Christ has served as a primary symbol of the connection between earth and heaven throughout Christian history.[1] The biblical image of Sophia also connects the Creator and the created. By restoring the biblical connection between Christ and Sophia, we strengthen the biblical imperative to care for God's creation, both human and non-human.

The image of Sophia with its connotations of the feminine divine is invaluable for theological discourse in that it is rooted firmly in biblical revelation. Although often ambiguous, undeveloped, and never fully formed, the image of Christ-Sophia is nevertheless present in the scriptures.[2] The presence of Sophia in the Hebrew and Christian Scriptures also provides contemporary spirituality with a figure of great possibility. Alas, traditional theology has almost totally destroyed the image of Sophia. Patriarchal religion has crucified Sophia. Sophia holds great promise, but requires resurrection if that promise is to be fulfilled.

Although the Christian church down through the centuries has affirmed belief in the resurrection of Christ, too often it has kept Christ entombed in dead traditions and rigid dogmas. Through resistance to change, the church has stifled the new creation inaugurated by the resurrection. The resurrection holds great promise that has never been fully realized. Jesus challenged followers to claim the power of the resurrection: "The one who believes in me will also do the works that I do and, in fact, will do greater works than these" (Jn 14:12). Bringing the resurrected Sophia and the resurrected Christ together promises not only further development of the feminine image of divinity, but also a fuller experience of the resurrection.

Including the female Sophia in the Christ-figure affirms women, men, and all creation in new and extraordinary ways. Christ-Sophia can help women claim power as their right, exercise it creatively, and share it. An exclusively male God cannot afford women this strength and independence.[3] Christ-Sophia can help men to affirm the importance and goodness of the nurturer within them and to value everything Western culture has disparaged as "feminine." Christ-Sophia can help all humankind to claim creative power and to take a prophetic role in righting wrongs against human beings and the rest of creation.

A church in the conservative Bible Belt had begun discussing inclusive language as a means of expanding concepts of God. Suggestions for changing language used in worship and education met strong resistance. The discussion became heated as traditionalists accused those in favor of inclusive language of tampering with the Word of God and destroying the beauty of familiar hymns. They also argued for keeping traditional language to avoid confusing children. The group for inclusiveness made an equally impassioned plea for the children. Inclusive language, they argued, was imperative for the development of an inclusive theology and an egalitarian church for their daughters and sons. Finally one member walked authoritatively to the pulpit. He angrily spouted out every argument he could muster against inclusive language. Then leaning over the pulpit with eyes glaring and finger pointed, he delivered what he considered the crowning blow: "And Jesus was a man! None of you can dispute that."

A similar objection, raised in a more peaceful tone, came from a chaplain at a retreat on the subject of "Feminist Theology and Pastoral Care." The chaplain said that his main problem in imaging God as inclusive of the feminine was his belief that Christ and God are one and that Christ is male. He could not get beyond his belief that the maleness of the historical Jesus made Christ eternally male. To many conservative Christians, an exclusively male Christ stands as a barrier to inclusive language and egalitarian church communities. For many feminists, an exclusively male Christ forms a block to the Christian faith in general. This book presents an inclusive christology that has the possibility of speaking both to traditionalists and feminists. It invites discovery of "the Power of God and the Wisdom [Sophia] of God" (1 Cor 1:24) through Christ-Sophia. Christ-Sophia gives us wisdom to expand our concepts of God and power to participate in resurrection.

One of the worship services in chapter eight of this book calls for the rethinking of Advent to include the coming of Christ-Sophia. Epiphany celebrations likewise provide an opportunity for the revisioning of Christ. Almost two thousand years ago, Wisdom's children called "Magi" received a revelation of the divine nature of

Jesus. Today wise women and men are receiving revelations of the inclusive nature of Christ-Sophia. Just as Advent goes beyond a one-time event to affirm continual comings of Christ-Sophia, the Epiphany continues to open our eyes to new revelations. We need the Epiphany to remove the blinders of exclusively masculine christology so that the light of Christ-Sophia can shine through. Christ-Sophia brings new revelations.

Christ-Sophia reveals the feminine face of God so long covered under layers of patriarchal theology. Christ-Sophia calls for further discovery and development of the biblical image of the eternal Sophia and of other feminine images of the divine in scripture. Christ-Sophia brings fuller revelation of the feminism of the historical Jesus. Recognition that Jesus incarnated Christ-Sophia sheds new light on Jesus' feminist words and actions. Christ-Sophia reveals the potential of the resurrection and the full meaning of new creation: "So if anyone is in Christ, there is a new creation: everything old has passed away; see, everything has become new!" (2 Cor 5:17). The new linguistic designation, "Christ-Sophia," symbolizes the extent of the new creation. Everything becomes new, including our language. Our new language in turn creates other new realities. The name "Christ-Sophia" expresses the ideal of new life for everything and everybody.

The resurrected Christ-Sophia gives us the ideal. The journey toward the ideal continues. Along the way, Christ-Sophia opens our eyes to new and creative possibilities for our spirituality. Through discovery of the Christ-Sophia within each one of us, we find the freedom to work in solidarity with oppressed sisters and brothers. Through this process we claim the love and power of the resurrected Christ-Sophia to bring change. We experience the enriching gifts of diversity as we strive toward a holistic Body of Christ-Sophia. Our spirituality becomes deeper and more fulfilling as we create new, life-changing worship experiences.

This is not the end but the beginning. The search for the resurrected Christ-Sophia goes on. Christ-Sophia invites all believers to join the quest. Christ-Sophia empowers us to participate in transforming oppressive theologies, rituals, individuals, and institutions into new, life-giving creations. The resurrected Christ-Sophia calls us to be co-creators of new life.

Notes

Introduction
1. Diane Tennis, *Is God The Only Reliable Father?* (Philadelphia: Westminster Press, 1985), p. 103.
2. Brian Wren, *What Language Shall I Borrow? God-Talk in Worship: A Male Response to Feminist Theology* (New York: Crossroad, 1990), p. 179.
3. Miriam Therese Winter, *WomanPrayer, WomanSong* (Bloomington, IN: Meyer-Stone Books, 1987), p. 7.
4. Saint Thomas Aquinas, *Summa Theologica*, trans. Edmund Hill (London: Blackfriars, 1964) Part 1, Q 92, 1 and 2; Q 99, 2, pp. 35-40, 165-67.
5. Naomi R. Goldenberg, *Changing of the Gods: Feminism and the End of Traditional Religions* (Boston: Beacon Press, 1979), p. 22.
6. Sandra M. Schneiders, *Women and the Word* (Mahwah, NJ: Paulist Press, 1986), p. 7.
7. Albert Schweitzer, *The Quest of the Historical Jesus* (London: A. & C. Black, 1926), p. 7.
8. All biblical references are to the New Revised Standard Version, unless otherwise noted.
9. Schweitzer, *The Quest of the Historical Jesus*, p. 399.
10. Matthew Fox, *The Coming of the Cosmic Christ* (San Francisco: HarperSanFrancisco, 1988), p. 162. Although Schweitzer's "Spirit of Jesus" and Fox's "Cosmic Christ" are not theologically synonymous, they both compel compassionate commitment to creation, resulting in social change.
11. Tom Driver, *Christ in a Changing World: Toward an Ethical Christology* (New York: Crossroad, 1981), p. 143.
12. Daniel L. Migliore, *Faith Seeking Understanding* (Grand Rapids, MI: Eerdmans, 1991), pp. 140-41.
13. Sacred Congregation for the Doctrine of the Faith, "Declaration on the Question of the Admission of Women to the Ministerial Priesthood," *Vatican Council II: More Postconciliar Documents*, ed. Austin Flannery (Collegeville, MN: Liturgical Press, 1982), p. 339.
14. Anselm, "Oratio LXV ad Sanctum Paulum Apostolum," *Opera Omnia, Patrologia Latina*, ed. J.P. Migne, vol. 158 (Paris, 1863), cols. 981-82. Julian of Norwich, *Revelations of Divine Love*, ed. Dom Roger Hudleston (London: Burns & Oates, 1927), p. 119. Aquinas, *Summa Theologica*, trans. R.J. Batten, Q. 34, 2a, 23, 2, p. 13. Although Aquinas believed that the female was by nature defective, he could not ignore the biblical connection between Christ and feminine Wisdom. This contradiction seems to have escaped him.

Chapter 1: Who Is Christ-Sophia?
1. Elizabeth A. Johnson, *She Who Is: The Mystery of God in Feminist Theological Discourse* (New York: Crossroad, 1992), pp. 87-89.
2. *Ibid.*, p. 95. See Johnson's incisive biblical exposition of the link between

Jesus and Sophia, pp. 94-100.
3. Joan Chamberlain Engelsman, *The Feminine Dimension of the Divine* (Philadelphia: Westminster Press, 1979), p. 140.
4. Elisabeth and Jurgen Moltmann, "Who Do You Say That I Am?" *Reformed World* 40 (December, 1989), p. 190.
5. Rosemary Radford Ruether, *Womanguides: Readings Toward a Feminist Theology* (Boston: Beacon Press, 1985), pp. 105-06.
6. See Jann Aldredge Clanton, *In Whose Image? God and Gender* (New York: Crossroad, 1990), pp. 96-98.
7. Elinor Lenz and Barbara Myerhoff, *The Feminization of America* (Los Angeles: Jeremy P. Tarcher, Inc., 1985), p. 237.
8. Rosabeth Moss Kanter, *When Giants Learn to Dance: Mastering the Challenges of Strategy, Management, and Careers in the 1990s* (New York: Simon and Schuster, 1989), p. 352.
9. Elisabeth Schüssler Fiorenza, *In Memory of Her: A Feminist Theological Reconstruction of Christian Origins* (New York: Crossroad, 1983), p. 102.
10. *Ibid.*, p. 190.
11. Anne E. Carr, *Transforming Grace: Christian Tradition and Women's Experience* (San Francisco: HarperSanFrancisco, 1988), pp. 172-77.
12. Marjorie Suchocki, "The Challenge of Mary Daly," *Encounter* 41 (Autumn, 1980), pp. 312-13.

Chapter 2: Christ-Sophia from the Beginning
1. The word "Christ" means "Messiah," or "Anointed One." See Isaiah 61:1.
2. Neil R. Lightfoot, *Jesus Christ Today: A Commentary on the Book of Hebrews* (Grand Rapids, MI: Baker Book House, 1976), p. 216.
3. James D.G. Dunn, *Christology in the Making: A New Testament Inquiry into the Origins of the Doctrine of the Incarnation* (Philadelphia: Westminster Press, 1980), pp. 206-10.
4. The Hebrew word translated "Wisdom" in the Hebrew Bible is *Hokmah*, which, like *Sophia*, is feminine gender.
5. References to the books of Wisdom and Ecclesiasticus (Sirach) are taken from the Jerusalem Bible.
6. Johnson, *She Who Is: The Mystery of God in Feminist Theological Discourse*, p. 89.
7. Susan Cady, Marian Ronan, and Hal Taussig, *Sophia: The Future of Feminist Spirituality* (San Francisco: Harper & Row, 1988), p. 49.
8. Marinus de Jonge, *Christology in Context: The Earliest Christian Response to Jesus* (Philadelphia: Westminster Press, 1988), pp. 121-22.
9. Fiorenza, *In Memory of Her*, pp. 130-35.
10. James M. Robinson, "Jesus as Sophos and Sophia: Wisdom Tradition and the Gospels," in *Aspects of Wisdom in Judaism and Early Christianity*, ed. Robert L. Wilken (Notre Dame, IN: University of Notre Dame Press, 1975), pp. 11-12.
11. James M. Robinson, "'Logoi Sophon': On the Gattung of Q," in *Trajectories Through Early Christianity*, ed. James M. Robinson and Helmut Koester (Philadelphia: Fortress Press, 1971), p. 104.
12. Rudolf Bultmann in *The History of the Synoptic Tradition*, trans. John Marsh (New York: Harper & Row, 1963), pp. 69-108, illustrates the close relationship between Jesus' sayings and Jewish wisdom literature.
13. Robinson, "Jesus as Sophos and Sophia," p. 11.
14. Jack M. Suggs, *Wisdom, Christology, and Law in Matthew's Gospel* (Cambridge, MA: Harvard University Press, 1970), pp. 66-71.

15. Cady *et al, Sophia,* p. 24.
16. Suggs, *Wisdom, Christology, and Law,* pp. 95-100. See also James M. Robinson, "Jesus as Sophos and Sophia," p. 10.
17. Dunn, *Christology in the Making,* pp. 201-02. James M. Robinson, in "'Logoi Sophon': On the Gattung of Q," pp. 112-13, concurs that this parallel between Luke 11:49–51 and Matthew 23:34–36 indicates the identification of Jesus with personified Wisdom.
18. Suggs, *Wisdom, Christology, and Law,* pp. 59-61.
19. See Suggs' thorough discussion of Matthew's identification of Jesus and Wisdom, pp. 31-130.
20. Felix Christ, *Jesus Sophia: Die Sophia-Christologie bei den Synoptikern* (Zurich: Buchdruckerei Meier & Cie, Schaffhausen, 1970), p. 80. By bringing the names "Jesus" and "Sophia" together in the title of his book, Felix Christ symbolizes their inseparability.
21. Dunn, *Christology in the Making,* pp. 213-14.
22. Jaroslav Pelikan, *Jesus Through the Centuries* (New Haven: Yale University Press, 1985), p. 59.
23. Glenn F. Chesnut, *Images of Christ: An Introduction to Christology* (Minneapolis: Seabury Press, 1984), pp. 38-49.
24. Pelikan, *Jesus Through the Centuries,* pp. 62-65.
25. Joseph E. Monti, *Who Do You Say That I Am?* (Mahwah, NJ: Paulist Press, 1984), p. 32.
26. Engelsman, *The Feminine Dimension of the Divine,* pp. 74-120, 139-148. Engelsman provides a thorough discussion of Sophia in biblical literature, and a plausible explanation of the way in which the misogynism of early theologians and the trinitarian controversies of the early church resulted in the repression of Sophia.
27. Tertullian, "Women's Dress," *Fathers of the Church,* trans. F.A. Wright (London: George Routledge and Sons, 1928), p. 52.
28. Dunn, *Christology in the Making,* pp. 213-14, 219.
29. Robinson, "Jesus as Sophos and Sophia," p. 6.
30. Pelikan, *Jesus Through the Centuries,* p. 58.
31. Dunn, *Christology in the Making,* p. 214.
32. See *Documents of the Christian Church,* ed. Henry Bettenson (London: Oxford University Press, 1963), p. 26.
33. Robinson, "Jesus as Sophos and Sophia," p. 9.
34. Gregory of Nazianzus, "The Third Theological Oration—on the Son," *Christology of the Later Fathers,* ed. E.R. Hardy, vol. 3 (London: SCM Press, 1954), p. 171.
35. Schneiders, *Women and the Word* , p. 3.
36. *Documents of the Christian Church,* p. 26.
37. *Book of Worship for Church and Home* (Nashville: The United Methodist Publishing House, 1964), p. 179.
38. Schneiders, *Women and the Word,* pp. 50-51.
39. Burton Cooper, "Metaphysics, Christology and Sexism: An Essay in Philosophical Theology," *Religious Studies* 16 (June, 1980), pp. 179-93. Cooper shows how Greek metaphysics abetted dualistic, patriarchal incarnational doctrines, and proposes a Whiteheadian metaphysic to underpin a non-sexist christology while strengthening incarnational faith.
40. Wren, *What Language Shall I Borrow? God-Talk in Worship: A Male Response to Feminist Theology,* p. 200.
41. Walter Kasper, *Jesus the Christ* (Mahwah, NJ: Paulist Press, 1976), p. 184. See Kasper's full treatment of Christ as "Son of God from Eternity," pp. 172-85.

42. Schneiders, *Women and the Word*, p. 55.
43. Justin Martyr, *The Works of S. Justin the Martyr* (Oxford: J.H. and Jas. Parker, 1861), p. 150.
44. Origen, *Commentary on John, The Ante-Nicene Fathers: The Writings of the Fathers down to A.D. 325*, ed. Allan Menzies, vol. 9 (New York: Christian Literature Company, 1896), pp. 317-18.
45. For a detailed discussion of the feminine images of God in scripture, see chapter 2 of Jann Aldredge Clanton, *In Whose Image? God and Gender* (New York: Crossroad, 1990), pp. 20-36.
46. Reinhold Niebuhr, *The Nature and Destiny of Man* (New York: Charles Scribner's Sons, 1941), p. 179.
47. Fox, *The Coming of the Cosmic Christ*, p. 21.
48. *Ibid.*, pp. 13-22.

Chapter 3: Christ-Sophia in the Flesh of Jesus
1. Edward Schillebeeckx, *Interim Report on the Books Jesus & Christ* (New York: Crossroad, 1981), p. 125.
2. Carr, *Transforming Grace: Christian Tradition and Women's Experience*, p. 98.
3. Ruether, *Womanguides: Readings Toward a Feminist Theology*, p. 108.
4. Rosemary Radford Ruether, *To Change the World: Christology and Cultural Criticism* (New York: Crossroad, 1983), p. 54.
5. Pauline Turner and Bernard Cooke, "Feminist Thought and Systematic Theology," in *Mainstreaming: Feminist Research for Teaching Religious Studies*, ed. Arlene Swidler and Walter E. Conn (New York: University Press of America, 1985), p. 57.
6. Linda Ellerbee, keynote address at "Calling All Women: To Celebrate Our Past and Embrace Our Future," sponsored by Liz Carpenter Lectureship in Humanities and Sciences, Ronya Kozmetsky Centennial Lectureship for Women in Management, Texas Union Distinguished Speakers Committee (Austin, TX, 1991).
7. Schneiders, *Women and the Word*, p. 62.
8. Leonard Swidler, *Biblical Affirmations of Woman* (Philadelphia: Westminster Press, 1979), p. 164.
9. Dorothy L. Sayers, *Are Women Human?* (Grand Rapids, MI: Eerdmans, 1971), p. 47.
10. Elisabeth Moltmann-Wendell, *Liberty, Equality, Sisterhood: On the Emancipation of Women in Church and Society*, trans. Ruth C. Gritsch (Philadelphia: Fortress Press, 1978), pp. 14, 19.
11. Aquinas, *Summa Theologica*, Q. 13, 1a, 12, 1, p. 37.
12. T.B. Maston, "The Bible and Women," *Light* (June, 1983), p. 5.
13. Evelyn and Frank Stagg, *Woman in the World of Jesus* (Philadelphia: Westminster Press, 1978), p. 118.
14. Ben Witherington, *Women in the Ministry of Jesus* (Cambridge: Cambridge University Press, 1984), p. 117.
15. See Mt 27:55–56,59–61; Mt 28:1; Mk 15:40–41, 45–47; Mk 16:1–2, 9; Lk 8:1–3; Lk 24:9–11; Jn 19:25–27; Jn 20:1–18.
16. Fiorenza, *In Memory of Her*, p. 329.
17. Elisabeth and Jurgen Moltmann, in "Who Do You Say That I Am?" pp. 179-93, discuss the crucial importance of Martha's confession, especially for the theology of resurrection.
18. Swidler, *Biblical Affirmations of Woman*, p. 193.
19. Mary Stewart Van Leeuwen, "Bread and Roses at Bethany," *Priscilla Papers* 5 (Spring, 1991), p. 2.

Notes

Notes 181

20. Kasper, *Jesus the Christ*, pp. 72-74.
21. Witherington, *Women in the Ministry of Jesus*, p. 40.
22. Proverbs 19:13.
23. Witherington, *Women in the Ministry of Jesus*, p. 36.
24. *Ibid.*, pp. 50, 125.
25. Swidler, *Biblical Affirmations of Woman*, p. 171.
26. See Swidler, p. 173, for a fuller interpretation of this passage, and pp. 164-73 for more detail concerning Jesus' feminist language.
27. Monti, *Who Do You Say That I Am?*, p. 21.
28. Patricia Wilson-Kastner, *Faith, Feminism, and the Christ* (Philadelphia: Fortress Press, 1983), pp. 77-78.
29. Schneiders, *Women and the Word*, p. 3.
30. Bill J. Leonard, "Forgiving Eve," unpublished sermon (July 29, 1984), p. 10.
31. Dallas M. Roark, *The Christian Faith* (Grand Rapids, MI: Baker Book House, 1969), p. 130. Also see *Documents of the Christian Church*, p. 45.
32. Wilson-Kastner, *Faith, Feminism, and the Christ*, pp. 30-90.
33. Fiorenza, *In Memory of Her*, pp. 100-279. See also Elisabeth Schüssler Fiorenza's *Discipleship of Equals* (New York: Crossroad, 1993).
34. Ruether, *Womanguides*, p. 109.

Chapter 4: The Risen Christ-Sophia
1. Shirley Jackson Case, *Jesus Through the Centuries* (Chicago: The University of Chicago Press, 1932), pp. 37-39.2.
   de Jonge, *Christology in Context: The Earliest Christian Response to Jesus*, p. 189.
3. *Ibid.*, pp. 115-16, 120.
4. Wilson-Kastner, *Faith, Feminism, and the Christ*, p. 91.
5. Jurgen Moltmann, *Theology of Hope* (New York: Harper and Row, 1967), pp. 165-66.
6. Kasper, *Jesus the Christ*, pp. 144-45.
7. Dunn, *Christology in the Making*, pp. 145-46, 159-61. See also de Jonge, *Christology in Context*, p. 117, for further discussion on the connection between the resurrection and the Holy Spirit.
8. Fiorenza, *In Memory of Her*, pp. 188-89.
9. Schillebeeckx, *Interim Report on the Books Jesus & Christ*, p. 75.
10. Winter, *WomanPrayer, WomanSong*, p. 7.
11. Kasper, *Jesus the Christ*, pp. 139-40.
12. Chesnut, *Images of Christ: An Introduction to Christology*, p. 135.
13. E. Glenn Hinson, *Jesus Christ* (Wilmington, NC: Consortium Books, 1977), p. 111.
14. Edward Schillebeeckx, *Christ the Sacrament of the Encounter with God* (New York: Sheed and Ward, 1963), p. 33-34.
15. Turner and Cooke, "Feminist Thought and Systematic Theology," pp. 57-58.
16. Lightfoot, *Jesus Christ Today: A Commentary on the Book of Hebrews*, pp. 5-6.
17. Hebrews 7:27; 9:12; 9:26; 10:10.
18. Paul W. Newman, *A Spirit Christology: Recovering the Biblical Paradigm of Christian Faith* (New York: University Press of America, 1987), pp. 171, 220, 214.
19. Rita Brock, "A Feminist Consciousness Looks at Christology," *Encounter* 41 (Autumn, 1980), pp. 325-26.
20. Fox, *The Coming of the Cosmic Christ*, p. 145.
21. Christin Lore Weber, *WomanChrist* (San Francisco: HarperSanFrancisco,

1987), p. 20.
22. *Ibid.*
23. See pp. 43-46 of Clanton, *In Whose Image? God and Gender.*
24. Weber, *WomanChrist,* p. 15.
25. Kasper, *Jesus the Christ,* pp. 154-56.

Chapter 5: Christ-Sophia Spirituality
1. Schubert M. Ogden, *The Point of Christology* (San Francisco: Harper & Row, 1982), pp. 39-40, refers to the "existential-historical" question, meaning that question not just about what has actually happened, but about its meaning for us here and now in the present, rather than about its meaning then and there in the past.
2. *Ibid.,* pp. 157-58.
3. Elizabeth Cady Stanton, *The Woman's Bible* (Seattle, WA: Coalition Task Force on Women and Religion, 1974), p. 12. *The Woman's Bible* gives a fascinating glimpse into the mind of a woman from the first wave of American feminism. Elizabeth Cady Stanton was the first to articulate the political nature of the Bible.
4. Fiorenza, *In Memory of Her,* pp. 3-36.
5. Mary Hembrow Snyder, *The Christology of Rosemary Radford Ruether: A Critical Introduction* (Mystic, CT: Twenty-Third Publications, 1988), p. 18.
6. See Clanton, *In Whose Image? God and Gender,* pp. 21-26, for a fuller discussion of images of God as Mother.
7. Ronda De Sola Chervin, ed., *Prayers of the Women Mystics* (Ann Arbor, MI: Servant Publications, 1992), pp. 123, 125.
8. Ruth Duck, "Sin, Grace, and Gender in Free-Church Protestant Worship," in *Women and Worship,* eds. Marjorie Procter-Smith and Janet R. Walton (Louisville: Westminster/John Knox Press, 1993), pp. 59-61.
9. Paul Smith, *Is It Okay To Call God "Mother": Considering the Feminine Face of God* (Peabody, MA: Hendrickson Pub., 1993), p. 203. For a thorough, incisive discussion of objections people raise to feminine language for God, see Smith's entire chapter 7, pp. 195-213.
10. Anselm, *Proslogium; Monologium; An Appendix in Behalf of the Fool by Gaunilon; and Cur Deus Homo,* trans. Sidney Norton Deane (La Salle, Il: Open Court, 1951), chapter 62, p. 105.
11. Plato, *Republic,* trans. B. Jowett, Book VII (New York: Modern Library, 1982), pp. 253-257.
12. Susan Cady, Marian Ronan, and Hal Taussig, *Wisdom's Feast: Sophia in Study and Celebration* (San Francisco: HarperSanFrancisco, 1989), p. 89. The entire sermon, pp. 89-93, "Sophia and Play" provides a non-threatening way of introducing the biblical figure of Sophia to congregations.
13. Fox, *The Coming of the Cosmic Christ,* p. 211.
14. Clarissa Pinola Estes, *Women Who Run With the Wolves* (New York: Ballantine Books, 1992), pp. 305, 308.
15. In *Women-Church: Theology and Practice of Feminist Liturgical Communities* (San Francisco: HarperSanFrancisco, 1986), p. 57, founder Rosemary Radford Ruether defines Women-Church as "the first time that women collectively have claimed to be church and have claimed the tradition of the exodus community as a community of liberation from patriarchy."
16. Daniel Goleman, Paul Kaufman, and Michael Ray, *The Creative Spirit* (New York: Penguin Books, 1992), p. 20.

Chapter 6: Christ-Sophia and Social Justice
1. Ogden, *The Point of Christology*, p. 167.
2. Ruether, *Women-Church: Theology and Practice of Feminist Liturgical Communities*, p. 28.
3. Lynn N. Rhodes, *Co-Creating: A Feminist Vision of Ministry* (Philadelphia: Westminster Press, 1987), p. 98.
4. Susan Thistlethwaite, ed., *A Just Peace* (New York: United Church Press, 1986), p. 58.
5. Martin Luther King, Jr., *Strength to Love* (New York: Harper & Row, 1963), p. 54.
6. This is a true story, but the names are pseudonyms.
7. Cady *et al*, *Wisdom's Feast*, p. 7.
8. See Gail Paterson Corrington, *Her Image of Salvation: Female Saviors and Formative Christianity* (Louisville: Westminster/John Knox Press, 1992), pp. 107-08; and Asphodel P. Long, *In A Chariot Drawn By Lions: The Search for the Female in Deity* (Freedom, CA: The Crossing Press, 1993), pp. 81-87. For a discussion of how Sophia blends black and white and transcends dualism, see Caitlin Matthews, *Sophia, Goddess of Wisdom: The Divine Feminine from Black Goddess to World-Soul* (London: Mandala, 1991), pp. 11-96.
9. Fiorenza, *In Memory of Her*, pp. 140-41.
10. Jeanne Achterberg, *Woman as Healer* (Boston: Shambhala Pub., 1990), pp. 3-5, 9-13.
11. Fiorenza, *In Memory of Her*, p. 141.
12. Fox, *The Coming of the Cosmic Christ*, p. 149.
13. Jacquelyn Grant, *White Women's Christ and Black Women's Jesus: Feminist Christology and Womanist Response* (Atlanta: Scholars Press, 1989), p. 216.
14. See the works of Toni Morrison, Zora Neale Hurston, Alice Walker, and Maya Angelou.

Chapter 7: The Church of Christ-Sophia
1. Turner and Cooke, "Feminist Thought and Systematic Theology," p. 58.
2. Schillebeeckx, *Christ the Sacrament of the Encounter with God*, p. 49.
3. Sacred Congregation for the Doctrine of the Faith, "Declaration on the Question of the Admission of Women to the Ministerial Priesthood," #5, in Flannery, *Vatican Council II: More Postconciliar Documents*, p. 339.
4. Schillebeeckx, *Christ the Sacrament of the Encounter with God*, p. 49.
5. Schneiders, *Women and the Word*, pp. 54-55.
6. Elisabeth Schüssler Fiorenza, *Discipleship of Equals: A Critical Feminist Ekklesia-logy of Liberation* (New York: Crossroad, 1993), p. 240.
7. Rhodes, *Co-Creating: A Feminist Vision of Ministry*, p. 29. From her experiences as a clergywoman and from interviews with other clergywomen, Rhodes presents new visions for the Christian community. She shows how feminist insights are changing the church's view of authority, salvation, mission, and vocation.
8. Carlyle Marney, *Priests to Each Other* (Greenville, SC: Smyth & Helwys, 1991), pp. 12, 14.
9. Katherine Zappone, *The Hope for Wholeness: A Spirituality for Feminists* (Mystic, CT: Twenty-Third Publications, 1991), p. 151. See Zappone's discussion of the creative possibilities of feminist ritual, pp. 149-59.
10. Fox, *The Coming of the Cosmic Christ*, p. 217.
11. See Lesley A. Northup, "Expanding the X-Axis: Women, Religious Ritual, and Culture," pp. 141-49, and Amitiyah Elayne Hyman, "Womanist

Ritual," pp. 173-81, in *Women and Religious Ritual*, ed. Lesley A. Northup (Washington DC: The Pastoral Press, 1993), for discussions of the use of experience in feminist and womanist ritual.

12. See the "Foreword," in Evelyn Eaton Whitehead and James D. Whitehead, *Community of Faith: Crafting Christian Communities Today* (Mystic, CT: Twenty-Third Publications, 1992), pp. v-viii.

13. See Ruether, *Women-Church: Theology and Practice of Feminist Liturgical Communities*, p. 88.

14. *Ibid.*, pp. 62-63.

15. Anne Anderson, "Dismantling Patriarchy—A Redemptive Vision: Ritual and Feminist Critical Theology in Basic Ecclesial Communities," pp. 183-97, in *Women and Religious Ritual*, ed. Lesley A. Northup (Washington DC: The Pastoral Press, 1993).

16. Whitehead and Whitehead, *Community of Faith*, p. 83.

17. Susan Brooks Thistlethwaite, *Sex, Race, and God* (New York: Crossroad, 1989), pp. 1-2, 109-120. This book provides a bold, thorough critique of white feminism, and proposes the examination of differences between the experiences of black and white women as a method of doing theology.

18. Grant, *White Women's Christ and Black Women's Jesus: Feminist Christology and Womanist Response*, pp. 212-20. White Christian feminists and black Christian womanists cannot overlook Grant's challenge toward a constructive, liberating christology through black women's tri-dimensional experience of racism, sexism, and classism.

19. "Response by Rosemary Ruether," in *Theology in the Americas*, ed. Sergio Torres and John Eagleson (Maryknoll, NY: Orbis, 1976), p. 373.

20. A black woman, leading a discussion on institutional racism, suggested that we use the term AHANA—acronym for Africans, Hispanics, Asians, Native Americans—instead of "minority," because AHANA is more specific and carries more positive connotations than the term "minority."

21. James H. Cone, *Martin & Malcolm & America: A Dream or a Nightmare* (Maryknoll, NY: Orbis, 1991), p. 109. See pp. 69-119 for fuller explanation of Malcolm's philosophy of separation.

22. Ruether, *Women-Church*, p. 57. See pp. 1-95 for a fuller discussion of the theological rationale for Women-Church.

23. "Response by Rosemary Ruether," *Theology in the Americas*, p. 373.

24. Frances W. Titus, *Narrative of Sojourner Truth* (New York: Arno Press, 1968), p. 132.

25. Quoted in Titus, *Narrative of Sojourner Truth*, p. 135.

26. *Ibid.*

27. Elizabeth Cady Stanton, Susan B. Anthony, and Matilda Joslyn Gage, *History of Woman Suffrage*, vol. 1 (New York: Fowler and Wells, 1881), p. 53.

28. Cone, *Martin & Malcolm & America*, pp. 274-80.

29. Martin Luther King, Jr., "I Have a Dream," in *A Testament of Hope: The Essential Writings of Martin Luther King, Jr.*, ed. James Melvin Washington (San Francisco: Harper & Row, 1986), p. 219.

30. Rosemary Radford Ruether, "Feminism and Jewish-Christian Dialogue," in *The Myth of Christian Uniqueness*, ed. John Hick and Paul F. Knitter (Maryknoll, NY: Orbis, 1987), pp. 146-47. Susan Brooks Thistlethwaite was team-teaching the class with Ruether in which the woman related this rape experience. Thistlethwaite relates this story in *Sex, Race, and God*, p. 93.

Chapter 8: Following Christ-Sophia Through the Seasons
1. *Meister Eckhart: A Modern Translation*, trans. Raymond Bernard Blakney (New York: Harper & Brothers, 1941), p. 95.
2. See Mariann Burke, *Advent and Psychic Birth* (Mahwah, NJ: Paulist Press, 1993), pp. 1-13.
3. Turner and Cooke, "Feminist Thought and Systematic Theology," p. 58.
4. Ruether, *Womanguides: Readings Toward a Feminist Theology* , p. 108.
5. Roberta Strauss Feuerlicht, *Madame Curie: A Concise Biography* (New York: American R.D.M. Corporation, 1965), pp. 30-43.

Chapter 9: Additional Worship Resources for Inclusive Communities
1. Written for Lisa A. Freeman, Earth Day 1990.
2. Adapted from Jane A. Keene, *A Winter's Song: A Liturgy for Women Seeking Healing from Sexual Abuse in Childhood* (NY: Pilgrim Press, 1991), p. 18.
3. Jacquie Clingan, "Ministry on Church Response to Family Violence" (Springfield, Illinois: Illinois Conference of Churches, 1989). Used with permission.
4. Marie Fortune, *Sexual Violence, The Unmentionable Sin: An Ethical and Pastoral Perspective* (New York: Pilgrim Press, 1983), p. 209.
5. Adapted from Ruether, *Women-Church: Theology & Practice*, pp. 171-72.
6. Keene, *A Winter's Song*, p. 25.
7. Words adapted by Sally Browder from *Child in the Manger* by Mary MacDondald; hymn tune *Bunessan*, a Gaelic Melody.
8. Adapted from Ruby Berkley Goodwin's "Black Madonna," in Cynthia Pearl Maus, *The World's Great Madonnas: An Anthology of Pictures, Poetry, Music, and Stories Centering in the Life of the Madonna and Her Son* (New York: Harper & Bros., 1947), pp. 451-52.
9. Words adapted by Sally Browder from "For All the Saints," by William W. How; hymn tune "Sine Nomine," by Ralph Vaughan Williams.
10. Words adapted from "This is My Father's World," by Katharine T. Babcock; hymn tune "Terra Patris," by Franklin L. Sheppard.
11. Words adapted from "Faith of Our Fathers," by Frederick W. Faber; hymn tune "St. Catherine," by Henri F. Hemy and adapted by James G. Walton.
12. Words by Edward Hopper; hymn tune "Pilot," by John E. Gould.
13. Phyllis Trible, *God and the Rhetoric of Sexuality* (Philadelphia: Fortress Press, 1978), p. 51.
14. Virginia Ramey Mollenkott, *The Divine Feminine: The Biblical Imagery of God as Female* (New York: Crossroad, 1983), pp. 89-90.
15. Words adapted from "Doxology," by Thomas Ken; hymn tune "Old," from the Genevan Psalter.
16. Adapted from Ruth Duck, *Flames of the Spirit* (New York: Pilgrim Press, 1985), p. 52.
17. Adapted from *Women's Prayer Services* edited by Iben Gjerding and Katherine Kinnamon, (Mystic, CT: Twenty-Third Publications, 1987).
18. Adapted from Miriam Therese Winter, "A Wisdom Psalm," *WomanWord* (New York: Crossroad, 1990), p. 33.
19. From the album "Medicine Music" (Hollywood, California: EMI-USA, Capitol Records, Inc., 1990).

Conclusion
1. Cady *et al*, *Sophia: The Future of Feminist Spirituality*, pp. 15, 80-82.
2. *Ibid.*, p. 54, 79, 86-87.
3. *Ibid.*, p. 83.

Index of Scripture References

ACTS (con't)	PAGE
4:33	53
4:34	61, 124
9:1–7	57
17:18	53
18:24—19:6	56

ROMANS	
8:9–10	55
8:19–23	59
8:22–23	89
8:26	72
12:4–8	99
12:5	96
16:25	20

1 CORINTHIANS	
1:23–24	10, 116
1:24	5, 20, 54, 56, 60, 174
1:30	20
2:7	20
8:6	20
10:4	20
12:4–27	99
12:27	5, 14, 96
15:3–5	40
15:14	53
15:17	4, 54
15:35–37	57
15:42–44	57

2 CORINTHIANS	
5:17	60, 175

GALATIANS	
1:12	57
1:15–17	57
2:4	68
2:19–20	67
2:20	55
3:27	20, 67
3:28	21, 31, 61, 68, 124
4:19	67

EPHESIANS	PAGE
3:10	20
3:18	23
4:4–16	99
5:22	37
6:5	37

PHILIPPIANS	
2:6–8	35
2:6–11	18
3:10	54

COLOSSIANS	
1:15	10, 31
1:15–16	18
1:15–17	18
1:16	19
1:17	19, 20
1:27	5, 14, 67

1 TIMOTHY	
2:11–12	37

HEBREWS	
1:1–3	18, 26
1:2	10, 19
1:3	10, 31
4:15–16	54
8:10	68
8:11	68
8:12	68
10:12	58, 68
11:1	78

JAMES	
1:5	115

1 PETER	
1:3–4	53
3:7	37

2 PETER	
1:4	30

REVELATION	
21:1–6	138
21:5	11, 15, 29, 60, 77, 127, 137
21:6	29

Of Related Interest...

The Hope for Wholeness
A Spirituality for Feminists
Katherine Zappone
The author emphasizes the necessity for women to develop relationships with themselves, others, God and nature in order to find a wholeness or completeness in their lives.

ISBN: 0-89622-495-3 208 pp, $12.95

Christianity and Feminism in Conversation
Regina A. Coll
Coll calls on readers to revise and reclaim the symbols, myths and metaphors of Christianity from a feminist perspective.

ISBN: 0-89622-579-8, 224 pp, $14.95

Jesus the Christ
Contemporary Perspectives
Brennan Hill
This book offers a solid, scripturally reliable and often surprising portrait of Jesus of Nazareth and the Christ of faith.

ISBN: 0-89622-492-9, 320 pp, $14.95

Available at religious bookstores or from
TWENTY-THIRD PUBLICATIONS
P.O. Box 180 • Mystic, CT 06355
1-800-321-0411